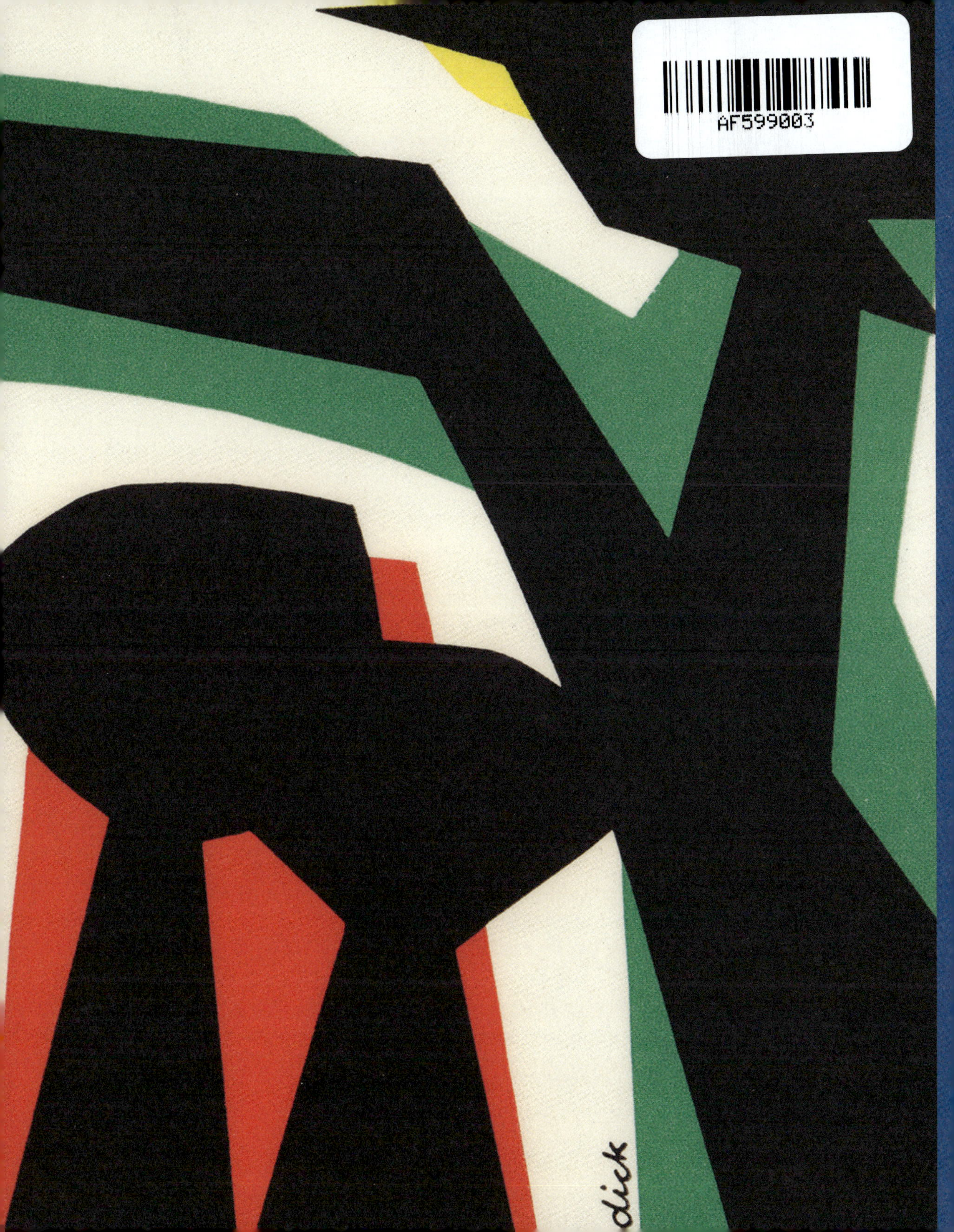
dick

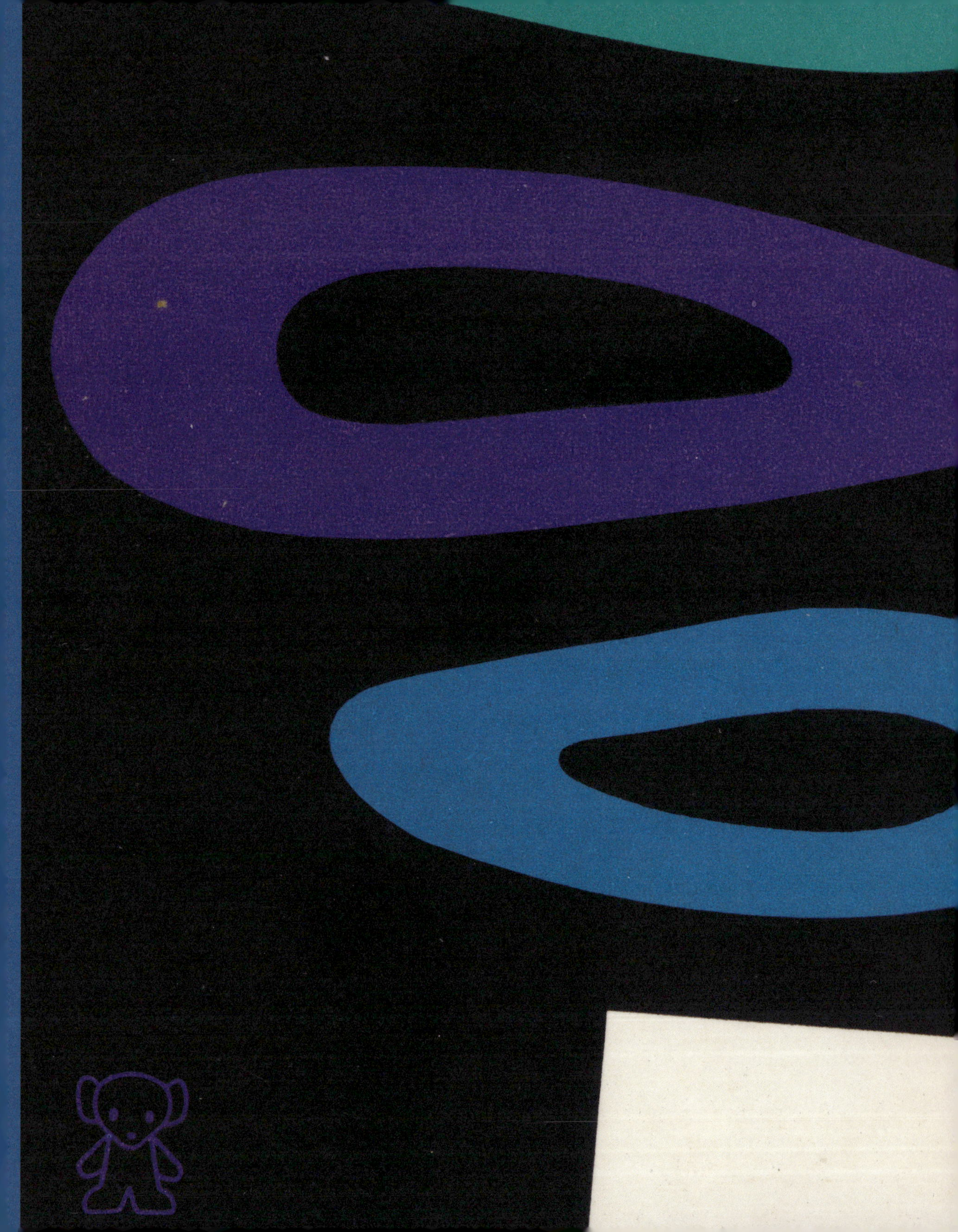

DICK BRUNA ARTIST

CARO VERBEEK

FOREWORD

It seems that for centuries Dutch artists have had an inner need to seek out the beauty that lies in the minutiae of everyday simplicity. We see it in Dutch landscape painting and in Vermeer, who captures a commonplace action such that the purity of the stilled moment is wholly poignant. We see this Dutch quality in Mondrian's compositions and in Schoonhoven's monochrome reliefs, distilled to an essence that any embellishment would destroy.

Dick Bruna understands, like the greatest Dutch masters, how to use simplicity to penetrate to the heart of the matter. His creations, Miffy above all, are a tour de force of telling minimalism. For sixty years Bruna drew a figure with pared-down actions and universally recognizable emotions. Over the years her *Gestalt* has changed imperceptibly. Each generation knows a different Miffy, an image that is not quite the same as that of their predecessors – she will have pointed ears for some, rounded ones for others. And yet her manifestation retains an iconic continuity. Miffy is constructed from monochrome planes of primary colours and clean lines. These lines describe the radical stillness, the small, the intimate. It is this purity that has for generations touched people all over the world and made Bruna's creations unassuming exemplars of what is so extraordinary about Dutch art and design.

In this exhibition and book, the Rijksmuseum explores the context in which his work was made. By placing his creations alongside those of his contemporaries, we shed light on their mutual influence and inspiration. Bruna combines the techniques of the colourful French avant-garde with the spare visual idiom of De Stijl. Looking at one of Bruna's works is like solving an art-historical puzzle: lines by Léger, colours by Rietveld, figures by Werkman.

The Rijksmuseum is most grateful to Dick Bruna and to Mercis bv for facilitating a long-term loan of a selection of Bruna's work in 2011. Curator Jacqueline de Raad (†) made the preparations for this by putting together a discerning selection that represents the full breadth and depth of Bruna's oeuvre, at the same time exploring the art-historical links with other artists. Curatorial project worker Caro Verbeek took her ideas forward for this book and exhibition, drawing on the Rijksprentenkabinet's superb collection of works on paper to illustrate for the first time the diversity of the associations with other artists. Thanks in part to the Centraal Museum in Utrecht, which endorsed the importance of Bruna's presence in the national collection in the Rijks-museum, we now house a group of works that assume their rightful place here, in the museum for Dutch art and history.

Dick Bruna. Artist sets Bruna's creative achievement within the international art-historical context of the twentieth century, and demonstrates the indispens-ability of his work in a collection that honours a cultural heritage beyond borders.

Wim Pijbes
General Director, Rijksmuseum

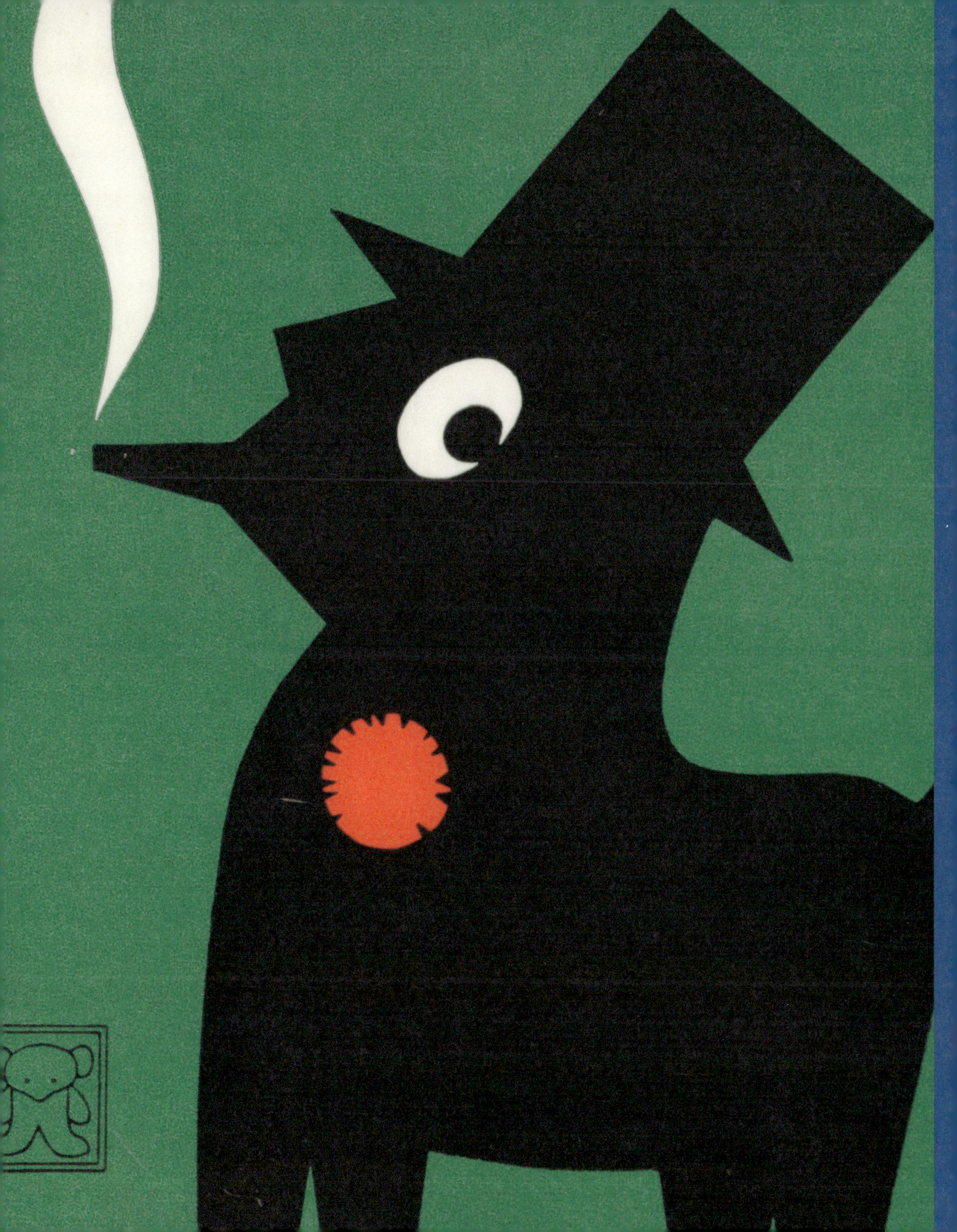

DICK BRUNA IN THE RIJKSMUSEUM

In the spring of 2011 Mercis bv placed 160 drawings, posters, prints and designs by Dick Bruna on long-term loan to the Rijksprentenkabinet, the print room of the Rijksmuseum. At the time the museum celebrated this event with an exhibition of designs from *de brief van nijntje* (*miffy's letter*) and a number of book covers [FIG. 1]. Four years later, to mark the sixtieth anniversary of Miffy's creation, the Rijksmuseum is showcasing the versatility of Bruna's work for the second time. The overview exhibition *Dick Bruna. Artist* presents highlights of a body of work that spans more than half a century, featuring drawings, designs, book covers and posters. But above all this exhibition shows how his work was inspired by modern art of the first half of the twentieth century. Although Bruna has often revealed his artistic sources in interviews, this is the first time that the art-historical leitmotif in his oeuvre is not only told, but also shown in detail, with his work hanging alongside that of his famous models.

Born in Utrecht in 1927, Dick Bruna is the son of the successful publisher A.W. Bruna. It was assumed that he would follow in his father's footsteps, but the young Dick Bruna had a more creative career in mind. Although he tried to study at the Amsterdam art academy, under family pressure to hurry up and make himself 'useful', he joined his father's publishing house as a designer of book jackets. Alongside his work as a cover designer, Dick Bruna also created autonomous work early in his career. In the early 1950s, for example, he produced still lifes and portraits of women in simple, uninterrupted lines, echoing the work of Matisse. In 1955, with the same simplicity and seeming ease, Bruna created a small rabbit. Not with a children's book in mind, but as a drawing to entertain his young son. She has meanwhile become one of the most famous rabbits of all time. He called her *nijntje*, a shortening of the diminutive *konijntje*, 'little rabbit'. The books featuring this character, who became Miffy in English, have been translated into more than fifty languages and are part of the collective memory of no fewer than three generations.

Perhaps because of his fame as the maker of popular children's books, Bruna has only relatively recently been 'museumized' and acknowledged as an artist with a capital 'A' in the Netherlands. He achieved this recognition a little earlier in other countries: the first retrospective of Bruna's work was staged in the Centre Pompidou in Paris in 1991. A serious presentation in the Netherlands followed five years later in the Groninger Museum, and the year after in Museum Boijmans Van Beuningen in Rotterdam. With the new millennium, it was the Utrecht Centraal Museum's turn. The Stedelijk Museum in Amsterdam – the national museum for design – had already begun to collect his posters in 1989, although the majority of the sixty works in its collection arrived after 2007.

Museums' burgeoning interest in Bruna's work is partly due to the growing appreciation of graphic design and applied art as fully-fledged art disciplines. Art historians increasingly recognize and acknowledge the modernist idiom and occasional applied art in Bruna's work. Hours of meticulous calculation, sketching and painting precede his deceptively simple designs. Craftsmanship, knowledge and individuality inconspicuously hide in the simple shapes.

Although art-historical connections are sometimes shrouded in mist and we can no longer ask the artists concerned, Bruna never made a secret of his main sources of inspiration. The French Purists, the Dutch De Stijl movement and several designers were among his most important models. We can see Matisse's cut-out compositions in his book jackets, Léger in Miffy's black outlines, Sandberg in his typography, Rietveld in the palette and the unusual, square shape of his book of prints. Bruna combines different influences to arrive at a unique and recognizable style. In the Miffy illustrations he seamlessly amalgamates French and Dutch Purism in a single image: an expressive (French) handling of line, set in geometrical, sometimes almost symmetrical (Dutch) shapes.

This publication sheds new light on a versatile designer and artist. With Miffy as the protagonist, the book outlines the international art-historical context that gave rise to Bruna's creations. We show that not only the book jackets that Bruna designed in his early years, but also our little heroine, are a legacy of the avant-garde. And yet it is, above all, Bruna's individuality that comes to the fore in these comparisons – and is celebrated in this book and exhibition.

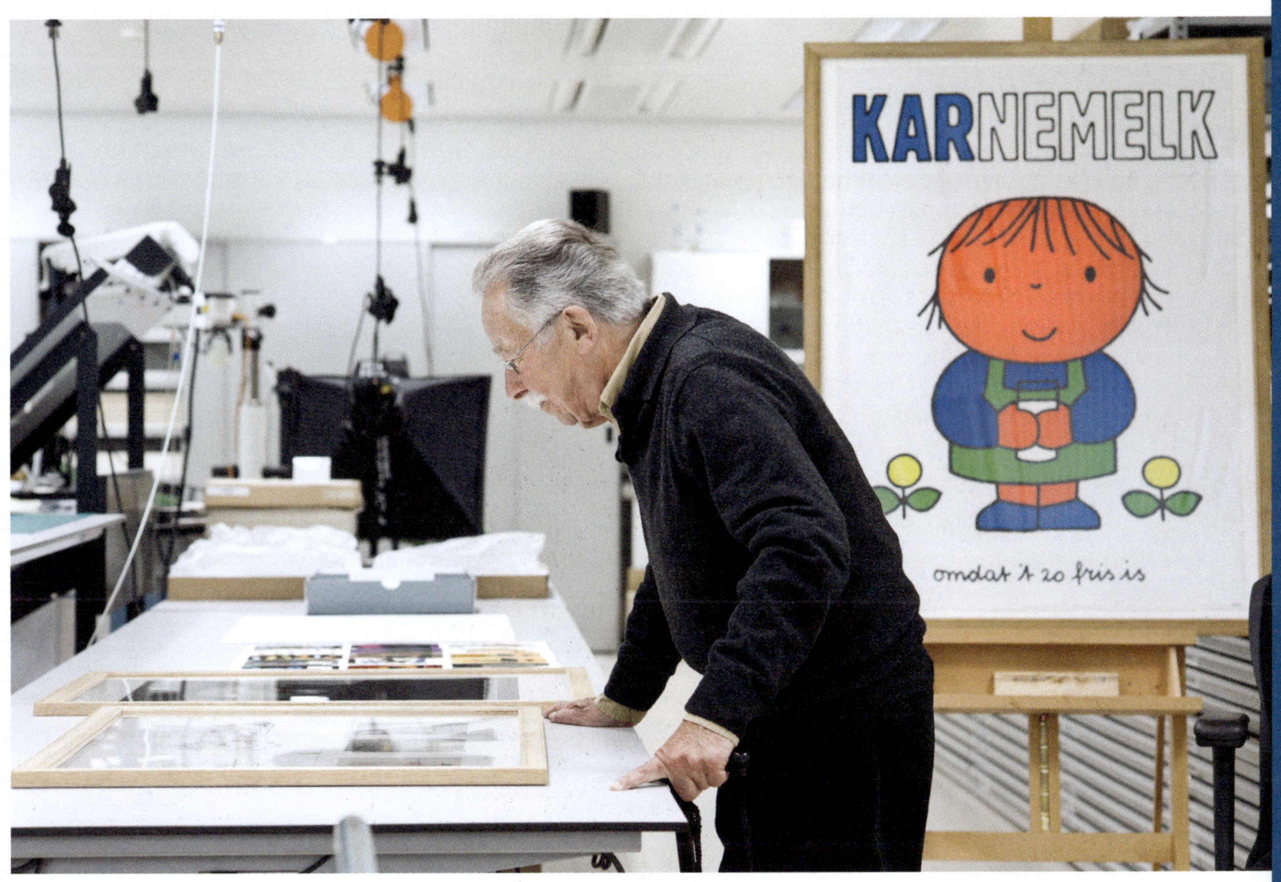

1 Dick Bruna during his visit to the Rijksmuseum restoration workshop in 2011

INSPIRATION

INTRODUCTION TO THE AVANT-GARDE: THOUSANDS OF 'ZWARTE BEERTJES'

Immediately after the war, under pressure from his father, the young Dick Bruna was sent to work in a publishing house in Paris. After all, as the oldest son he was expected to take over the family firm. Instead of devoting himself to business, Bruna seized every opportunity to visit museums and galleries, where he saw work by Henri Matisse, Fernand Léger and Pablo Picasso for the first time. Simple shapes, abstraction, convincing black lines, solid planes and bright primary colours characterize their work. The young man, who had only seen a book of pictures by Rembrandt and Vincent van Gogh, was amazed. It is then that he knew without doubt that he wanted to become an artist.

However, when he returned home from Paris, he met with resistance from his father. His future father-in-law likewise stood in his way, for he wished to prevent his daughter from marrying a penniless artist. With that, his father decided that his son should start by designing dust jackets for the books he published. Looking back, Bruna is grateful: 'This turned out to be a blessing. As an autonomous artist, I would never have been able to achieve a decent standard. The very constraints inherent in designing book covers were of crucial importance to me.'[1]

What began as a practical compromise became a period of freedom, experiment and lightning-fast creative development for Bruna. Between 1951 and 1969 he designed more than two thousand covers for the popular light-hearted detective series *Zwarte Beertjes* (Little Black Bears), published by A.W. Bruna & Zn. The publisher had a kiosk selling its books in every railway station in the Netherlands: no fewer than a hundred million copies were sold between 1951 and 1969. The breath-taking pace at which the *Zwarte Beertjes* are published compelled Bruna to use many different techniques, including cutting, tearing, pasting, photography, drawing, painting and collage. His style developed rapidly because of the necessity to experiment with different media.

The power of Bruna's jacket designs for the *Zwarte Beertjes* lies in the iconic images of the protagonists. On the covers of the Maigret series by Georges Simenon, for instance, there is always a pipe, and the characteristic silhouette of the *Schaduw* (Shadow) wears different hats and appears in a different manifestation every time [FIGS. 2A, B AND 3A, B]. The light-hearted diversity never detracted from the recognition factor: hurried travellers knew at a glance that the next part of their favourite leisure reading had been published. The simple pictorial idiom also makes the *Zwarte Beertjes* very appealing. In his book jackets, Bruna handled the balance between text and image very carefully, with pinpoint selectivity. At the same time he ensured that the image evoked the atmosphere of the contents of the book and aroused readers' interest without giving too much away: 'a book cover must not stand in the way of the reader's imagination'.[2] As the designer for the *Zwarte Beertjes*, Bruna learned how to stimulate a wide audience.

2A, B
Dick Bruna
cover design for
Georges Simenon,
Maigret en de gangsters
(*Maigret and the Gangsters*)
1970

Dick Bruna
cover for Georges Simenon,
De woede van Maigret
(*Maigret Loses His Temper*)
1964

3A, B
Dick Bruna
cover design for Havank,
Circus Mikkenie
1965

Dick Bruna
cover design for Havank,
De Schaduw is terug
(*The Shadow Returns*)
1966

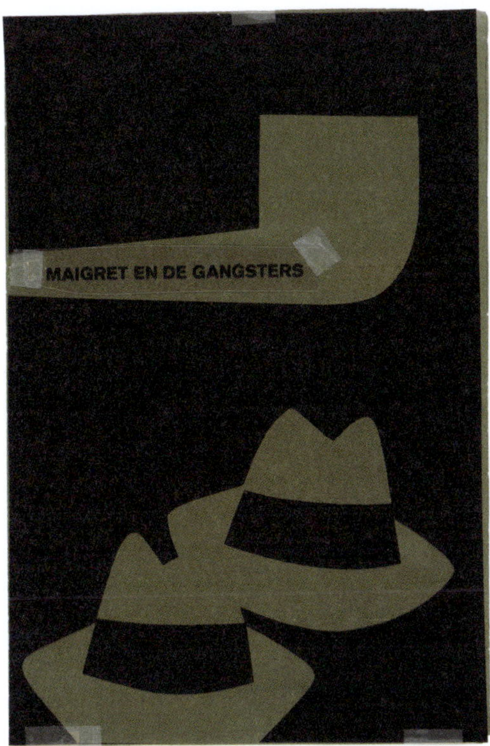
MAIGRET EN DE GANGSTERS

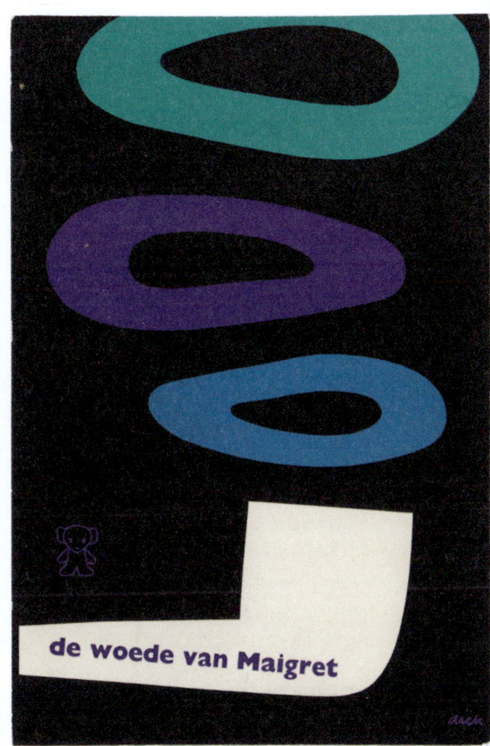
de woede van Maigret
dick

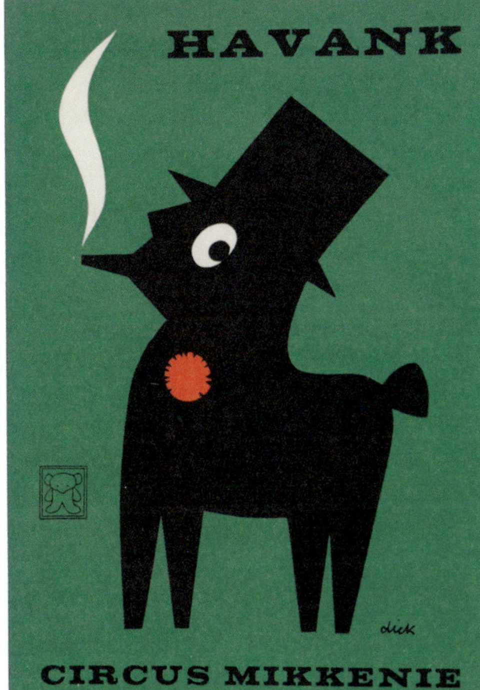
HAVANK
dick
CIRCUS MIKKENIE

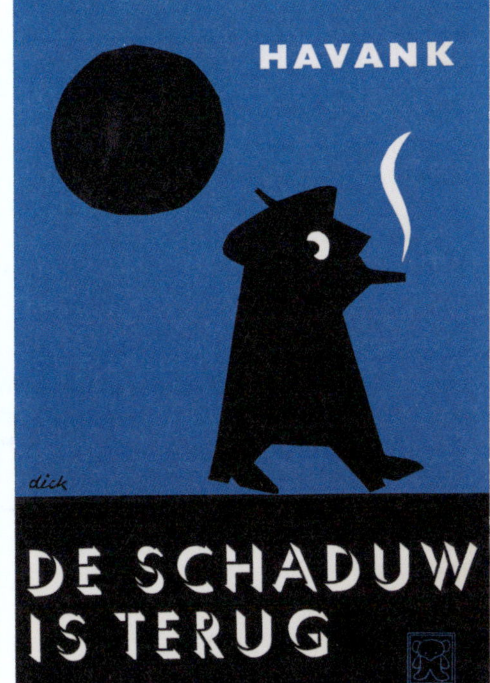
HAVANK
dick
DE SCHADUW
IS TERUG

The French Avant-Garde

For inspiration Bruna looked at the world around him, as well as back in time. Many of his designs for the *Zwarte Beertjes* are redolent of Paris in the first half of the twentieth century. They are inspired by movements grouped together as the historic French avant-garde, which emerged around 1916 and continued until the outbreak of the Second World War. The pre-war avant-garde movements in France were known for their experiments, innovation and deliberate stylistic breaks with the past.

The approach to composition, the simplification of form and the use of colour in Bruna's cover designs reflect above all the work of Henri Matisse (1869–1954), one of the protagonists of the French avant-garde. Bruna explains, 'I learned simplicity and the use of colour from Matisse. I thought those cut-outs made from solid colours on a white surface were fantastic. I took that further for the covers.'[3] In 1947 Matisse created the artist's book *Jazz* using these paper cut-outs [FIGS. 5A, B]. Bruna was overcome by the freedom and spontaneity it conveyed. He purchased a facsimile of the expensive work and drew inspiration from it for countless jacket designs.

Cut-out shapes regularly appeared in the *Zwarte Beertjes*, as in *Maigret aan de Rivièra* (*Maigret on the Riviera*) [FIG. 4]. Each of the red rooftops is a slightly different shape, creating a lively rhythm. The background is a meandering coastline from a bird's-eye view that conveys a sense of depth, but nonetheless looks 'flat' because of the lack of linear perspective and the fact that the buildings, trees and boats are shown from the front. This contradictory perspective is typical of the Cubists in the first decade of the last century, and was used by Georges Braque, Pablo Picasso and others. The composition, the simplicity of form, the amalgamation of foreground and background and the palette were more likely inspired by Matisse. In the design for *Weerzien op een plastichuid* (Reunion on a Plasticskin [*sic*]) by Lizzy Sara May, scissors were also used, but in an entirely different way [FIG. 6]. The shapes are more angular and geometric, strongly symmetrical, and the third dimension is entirely absent.

The cover Bruna designed for *Maigret en de geschaduwde schoolmeester* (*Maigret Goes to School*) by George Simenon is a tribute to the avant-garde artist Fernand Léger (1881–1955), one of Matisse's contemporaries who, like him, lived and worked in Paris. Bruna discovered the detachment of plane and line in Léger's work [FIG. 7]. He was captivated above all by the double perspective this creates: 'You can actually look twice. You see the lines, the pattern and the image, and behind them the colours are separate: then you have to look twice, which gives such a fine effect.'[4] This unusual interaction between planes of colour and outlines is also much in evidence in other work by Bruna, such as the poster *Vakantie met een boek* (Holiday with a Book) [FIG. 8]. Léger's bold black outlines return later in almost all of Bruna's work: in his book jackets and in his individual drawings, including Miffy.

4 Dick Bruna
cover for Georges Simenon,
Maigret aan de Rivièra
(*Maigret on the Riviera*)
1968

Maigret aan de Rivièra

Simenon

dick

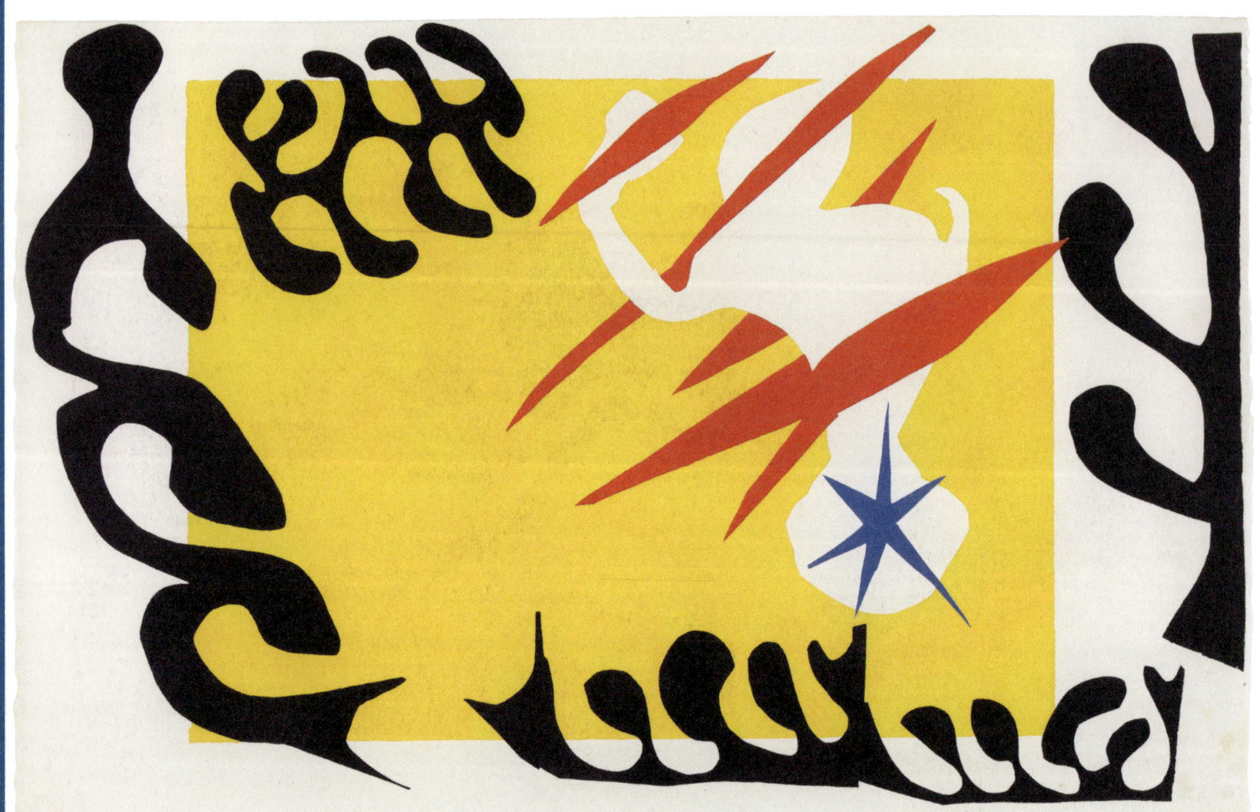

5A Henri Matisse
Jazz no. 4, The Nightmare of the White Elephant, pages in the artist's book *Jazz*
1947

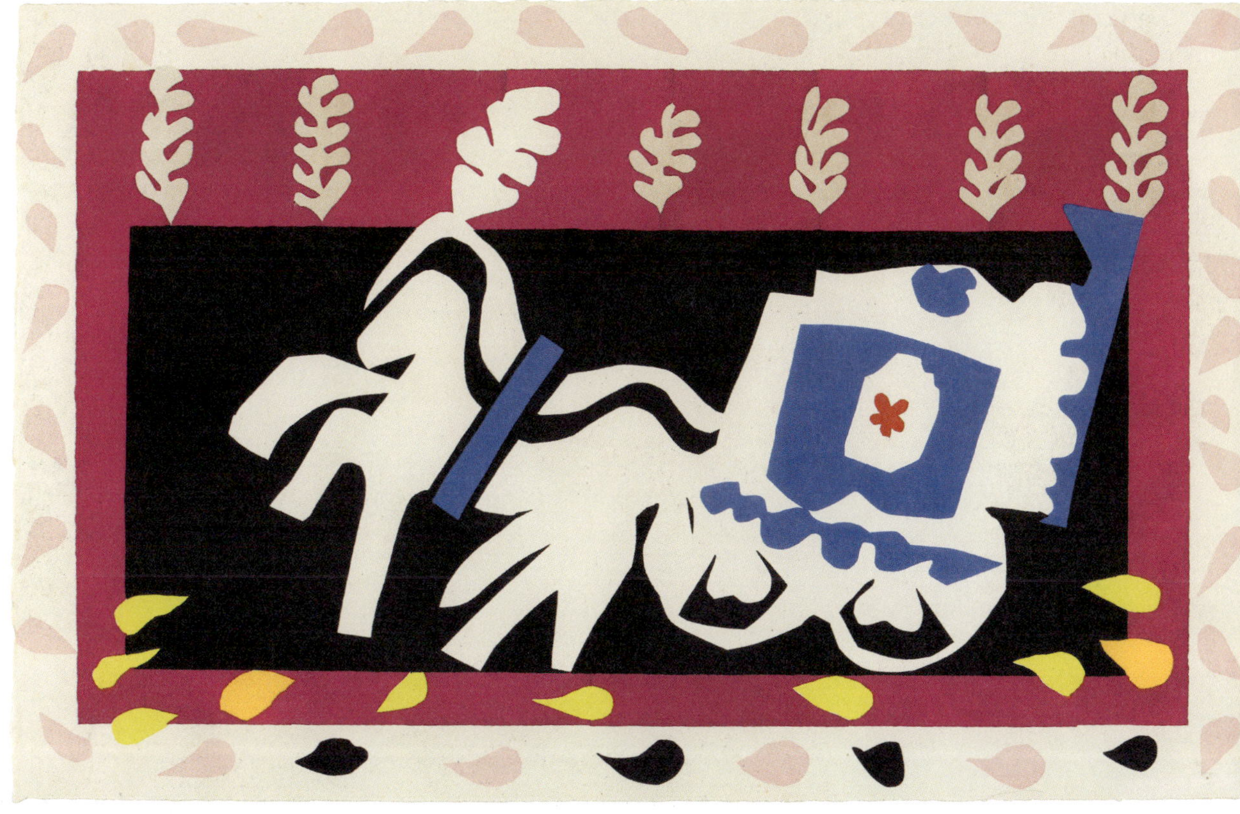

5B Henri Matisse
Jazz no. 10, The Funeral of Pierrot, pages in the artist's book *Jazz*
1947

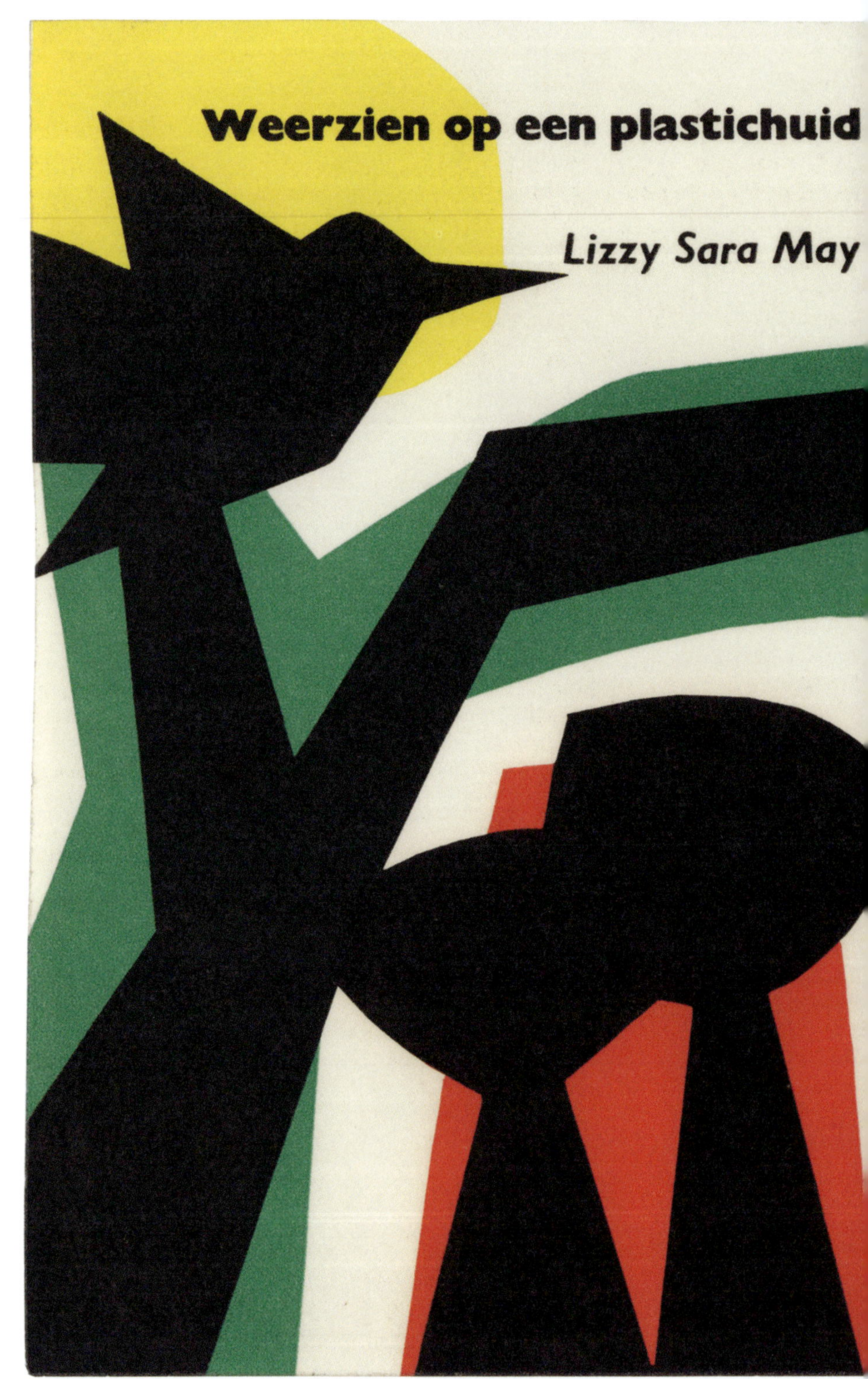

6 Dick Bruna
cover for Lizzy Sara May,
Weerzien op een plastichuid
(*Reunion on a Plasticskin*)
1957

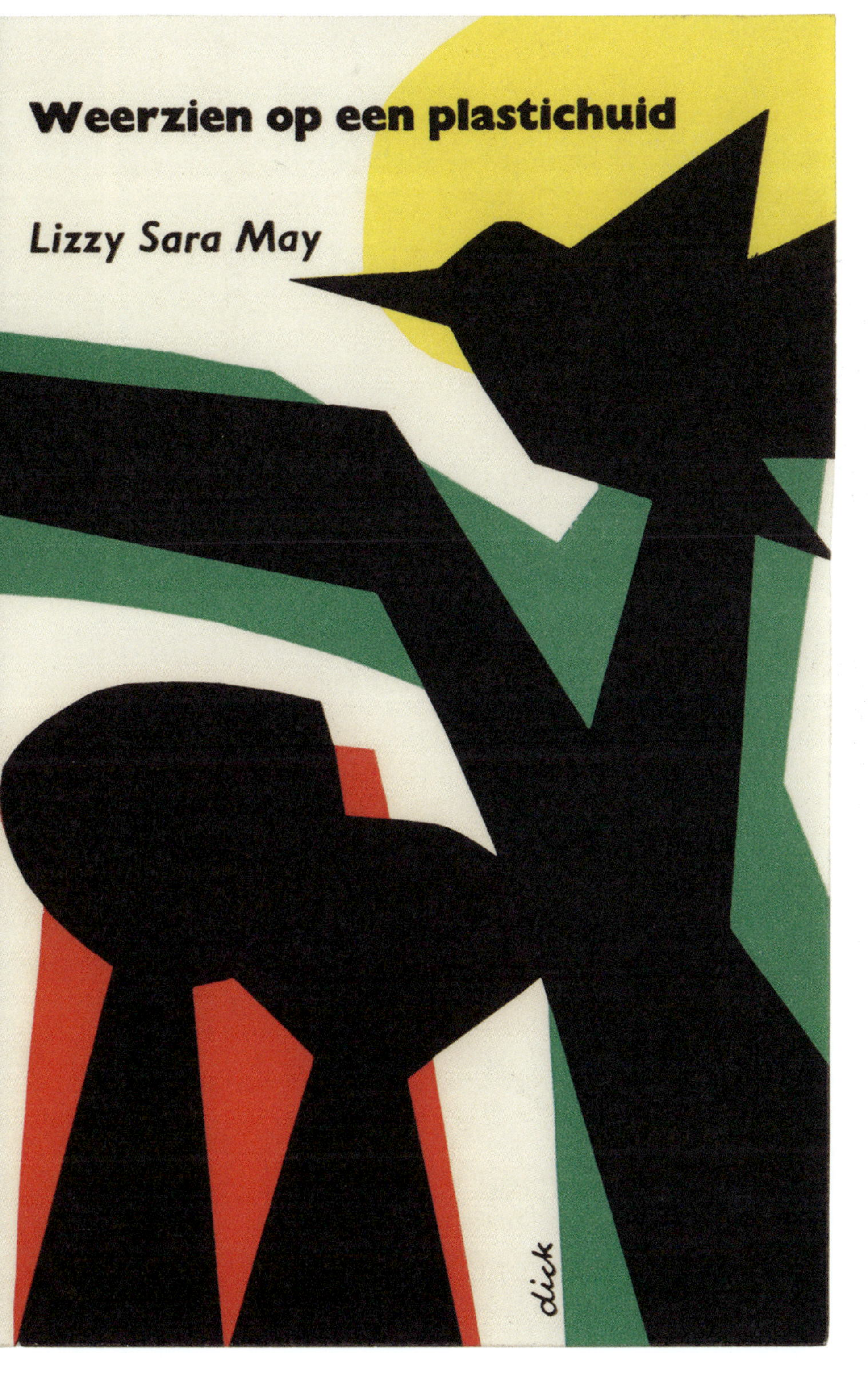
Weerzien op een plastichuid
Lizzy Sara May
dick

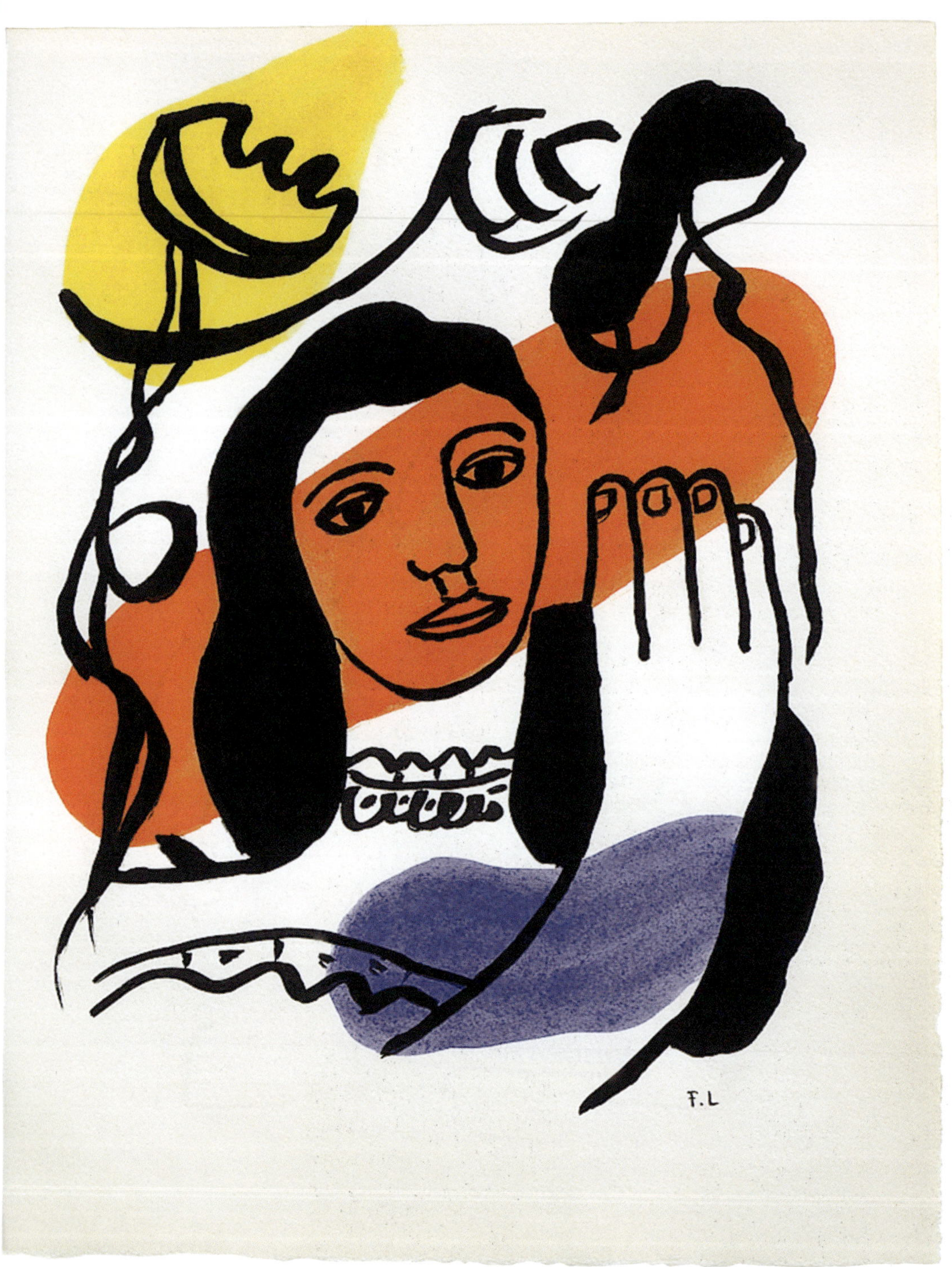

7 Fernand Léger
Fêtes de la faim,
in *Les Illuminations*
1949

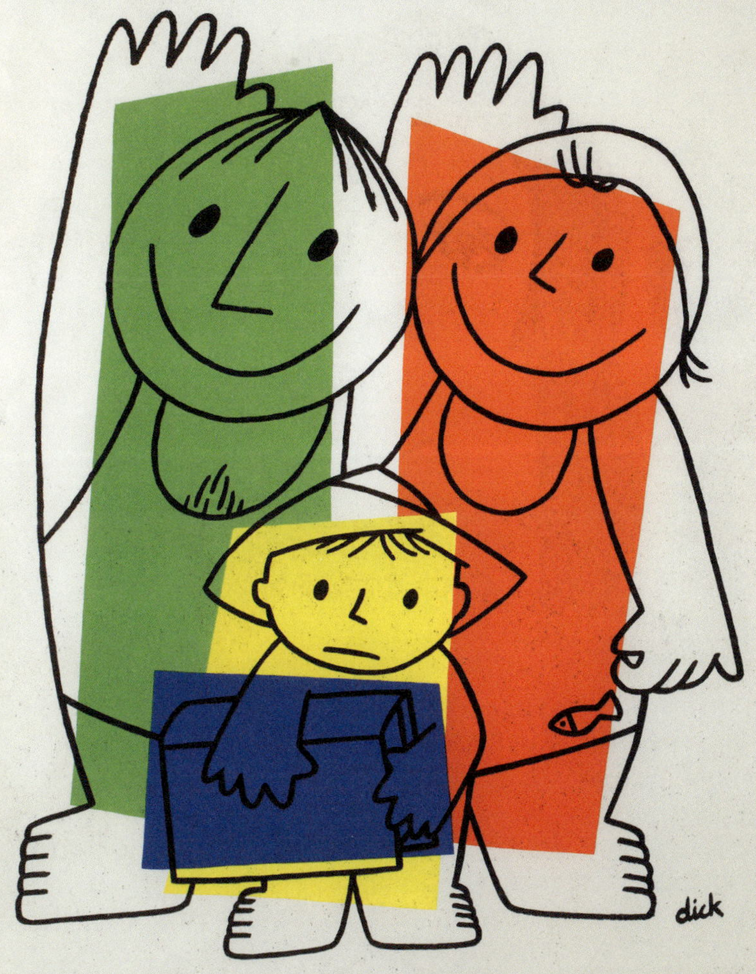

8 Dick Bruna
poster *Vakantie met een boek*
(*Holiday with a Book*)
1952

BRAMEN MET ARSEN

Sandberg

Bruna found a source of inspiration closer to home in the work of the designer, curator and museum director Willem Sandberg (1897–1984). From an early stage Sandberg followed contemporary art movements like CoBrA and – much to the great displeasure of the established order – gave them a platform in the Stedelijk Museum in Amsterdam, where after the war he dared to paint the walls white. As a designer, he employed a Modernist idiom, which, in terms of colour, typography and design vocabulary, was also based on the French avant-garde. His countless posters were conceived according to principles of simplicity and clarity, but it was above all his experiments with lettering that defined the image, made his work so innovative and appealed to many young designers. The torn lettering that Sandberg used in his designs had an unmistakable influence on Bruna's own.

On the cover Bruna developed for *Het boek IK* (The Book I) by Bert Schierbeek and *Steekspel in San Sebastian* (Dual in San Sebastian) by Joop van den Broek, the letters shape the composition [FIGS. 12A, B]. Their colour, size, position and the way they were cut out make the punctuation marks coincide with the design. Sandberg achieved the same effect in his famous design for the *Aanwinsten 1945–54. 9 jaar Stedelijk Museum* (Acquisitions 1945–54. 9 Years Stedelijk Museum) catalogue [FIG. 10]. A seemingly torn number '9' embellishes the cover. In Sandberg's renowned design for *Biblio*, the 'b's are created from a torn collage [FIG. 11]. In fact Sandberg used a needle to give the paint 'torn' fringes. This was a time-consuming task that was anything but spontaneous.

Bruna used pieces of paper that really had been torn in the design of the *Zwarte Beertjes* jackets for *Zij zou op het eiland tegen hem zeggen* (She Would Tell Him on the Island; published in French as *Elle lui dirait dans l'île*) by Françoise Xenakis [FIG. 13] and *Bramen met arsenicum* (*We Have Always Lived in the Castle*) by Shirley Jackson [FIG. 9]. The best use was made of the properties of paper: tearing left room for spontaneity and chance. Broken white paper fibres in the fringes fostered two-dimensionality. Bruna explained that 'what most appealed to me was that Sandberg did not use perspective'.[5] The source, the driving force behind this pictorial idiom was clearly Matisse, their shared example.

The similarities between Sandberg and Bruna did not, of course, stand in isolation. The post-war years saw a renewed interest in the style of the first half of the twentieth century and it was Sandberg who used the work of Matisse and his contemporaries as inspiration and also – as the curator and director of the Stedelijk Museum – made it accessible to the Dutch public. Bruna's pictorial language reflected the spirit of the time and was shared by many artists in this period.

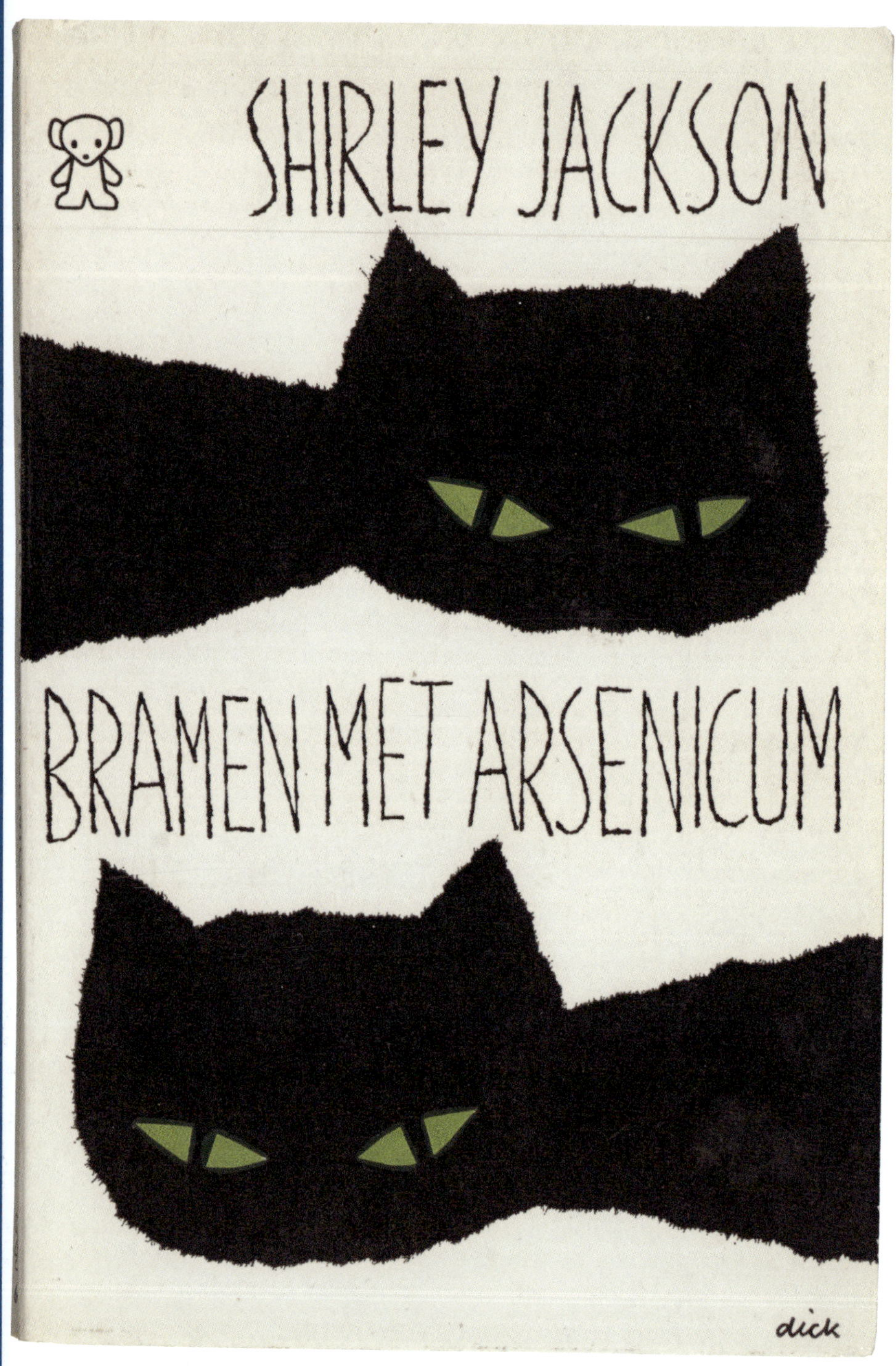

9 Dick Bruna
cover for Shirley Jackson,
Bramen met arsenicum
(*We Have Always Lived in the Castle*)
1963

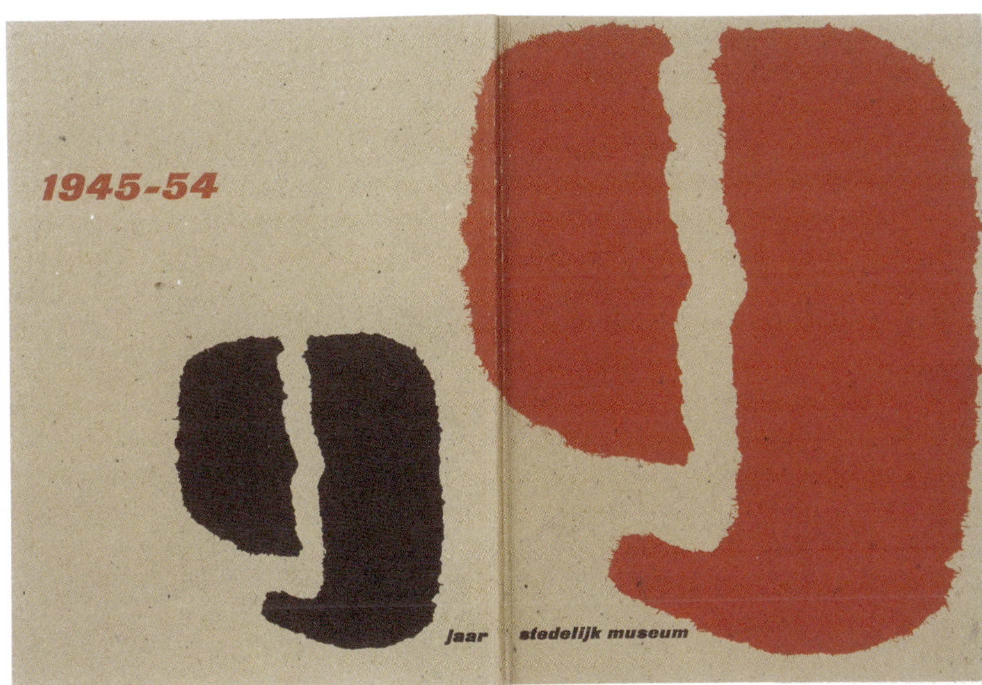

10 Willem Sandberg
cover for *Aanwinsten 1945–54. 9 jaar Stedelijk Museum*
(Acquisitions 1945–54. 9 Years Stedelijk Museum)
1945

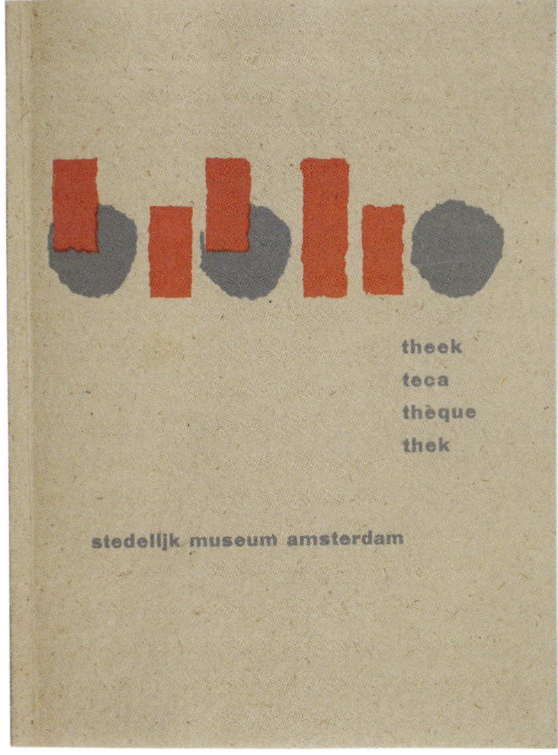

11 Willem Sandberg
cover for *Biblio*
1957

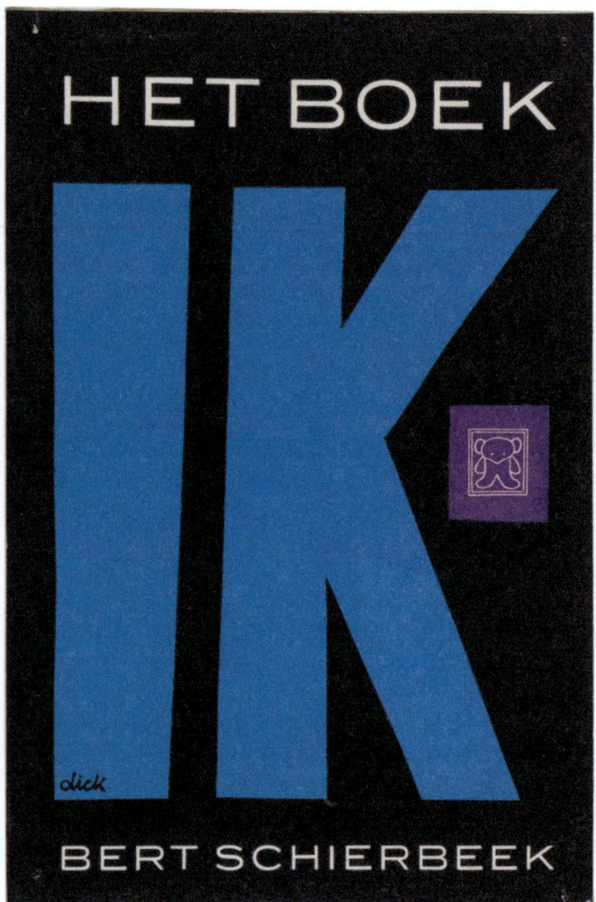

12A
Dick Bruna
cover for Bert Schierbeek,
Het boek IK (*The Book I*)
1960

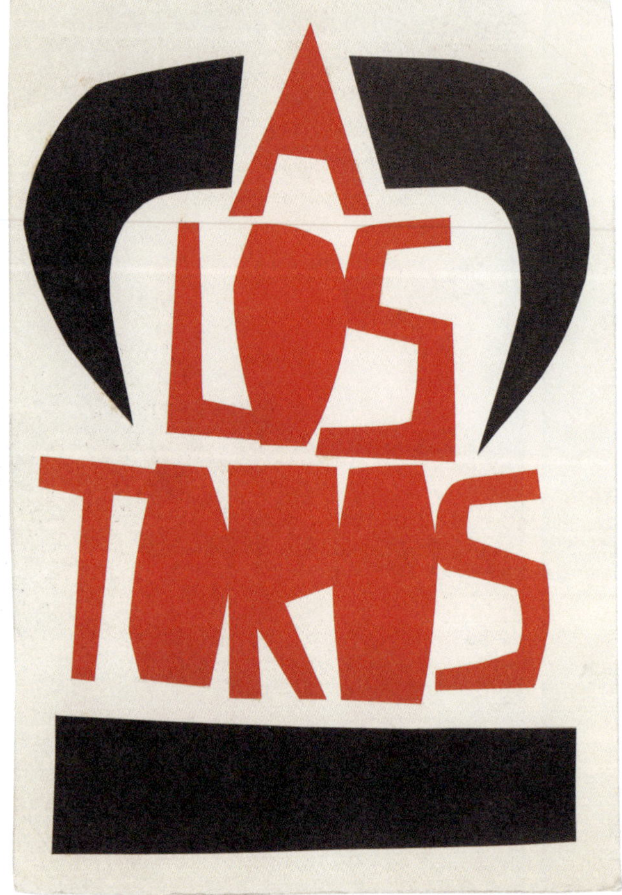

12B
Dick Bruna
cover for Joop van den Broek,
Steekspel in San Sebastian
(*Dual in San Sebastian*)
1961

13 Dick Bruna
cover for Françoise Xenakis,
Zij zou op het eiland tegen
hem zeggen (She Would
Tell Him on the Island)
1972

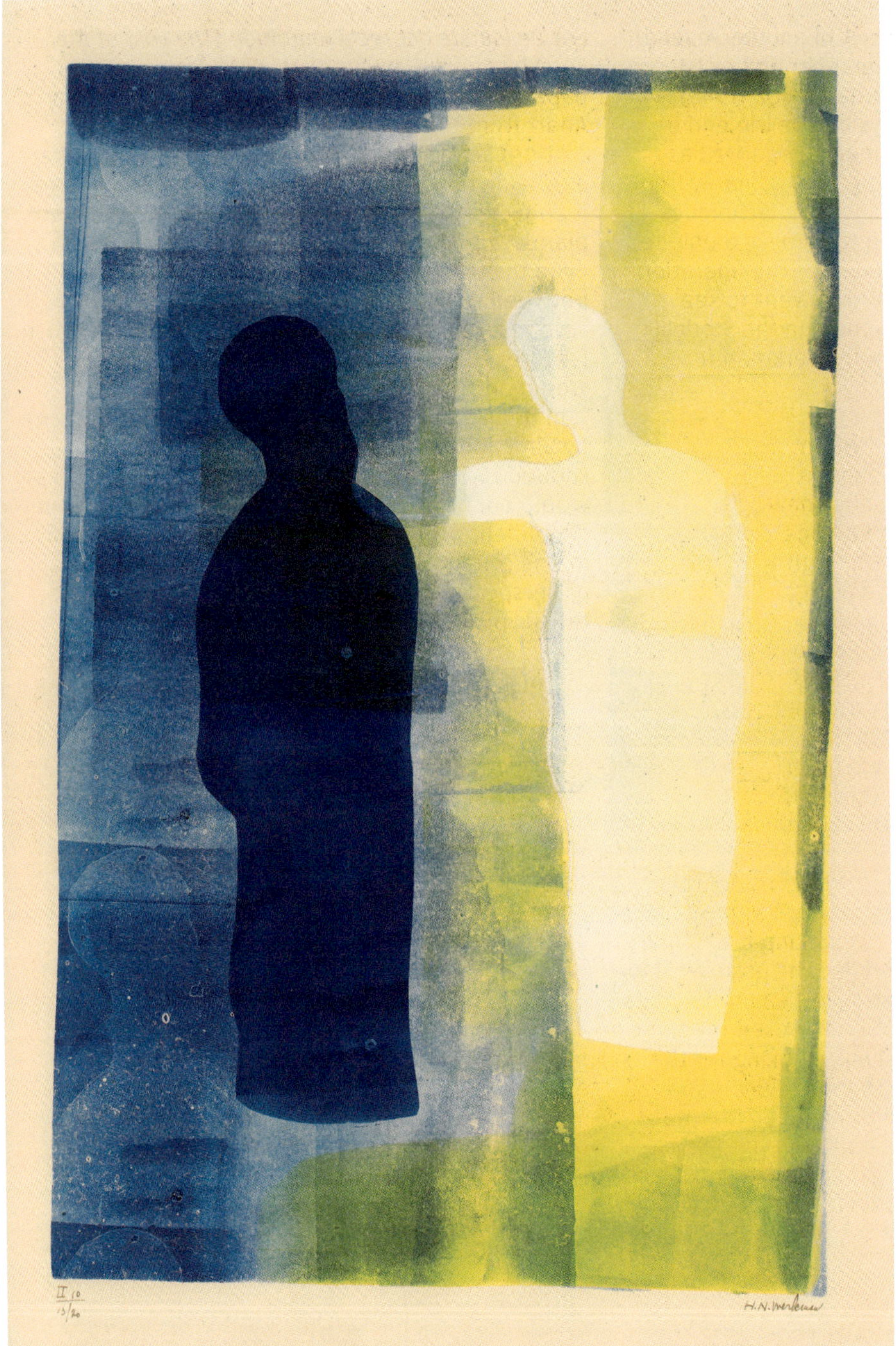

14 H.N. Werkman
Chassidische legenden II–10: De engel van den laatsten troost
(*Hasidic Legends II–10: The Angel of Ultimate Comfort*)
1941

Werkman

Sandberg put Bruna on the track of another legendary Dutch graphic artist, typographer and resistance hero, Hendrik Nicolaas Werkman (1882–1945), who was executed three days before the end of the Second World War. Werkman is regarded as the inventor of the '*druksel*': an extraordinarily free approach to printing, combining such techniques as rolling, stamping and stencilling to make a unique print or monotype [FIG. 14]. Soon after the liberation of the Netherlands in 1945, Bruna went to see an exhibition curated by Sandberg in the Stedelijk Museum, where he saw work by Werkman for the first time:

> 'I was eighteen years old when the war ended. We had been in hiding for two years. I really knew nothing. At home we had a book about Rembrandt and Van Gogh. That was all. It was only after a while that all kinds of things emerged about what happened here during the war. Then I saw those magnificent prints from Hendrik Werkman's *Hasidic Legends*. Those prints have been really important to me; they were totally direct and abstract things.'[6]

From 1935 onwards, Werkman would frequently use stencilling. He cut shapes out with a sharp blade in a fluent movement, without making preliminary sketches. Sometimes he just rolled the positive shape in with ink, sometimes he also worked on the negative shape with the roller. Werkman used the same negative template twice without re-inking for the figures in *Sabbatsgesänge* (*Sabbath Singing*) [FIG. 16], creating a visual echo in a lighter shade. The transparency and blurring create a three-dimensional effect that is strengthened by the table top. No fewer than three templates were used to make the menorah on the back of the pamphlet.

For *De laatste der rechtvaardigen* (*The Last of the Just*) by André Schwarz-Bart [FIG. 15], Bruna cut out paper silhouettes that are reminiscent of Werkman's. Apart from the similar method (snipping versus cutting) and the pictorial language itself, they share a certain plasticity of form. Bruna created this by overlapping the transparent figures and the staggered planes in pink and red that form the background. Even the theme of Jewish culture is a clear link between Werkman and Bruna. Bruna designed a second cover for André Schwartz-Bart's book, which features a menorah [FIG. 17], much like the one on Werkman's *Sabbatsgesänge*.

In Bruna's design for the cover of *De zoon* (*The Son*) by Simenon, we also see beings that have much in common with Werkman's direct iconic style. Werkman would not have been so quick to use black, but the simplified, whimsical figures without detail, applied in one colour or a few, as well as the abandonment of perspective without losing spatiality, are characteristic of them both.

ANDRÉ

SCHWARZ-BART

DE LAATSTE DER RECHTVAARDIGEN

BRUNA

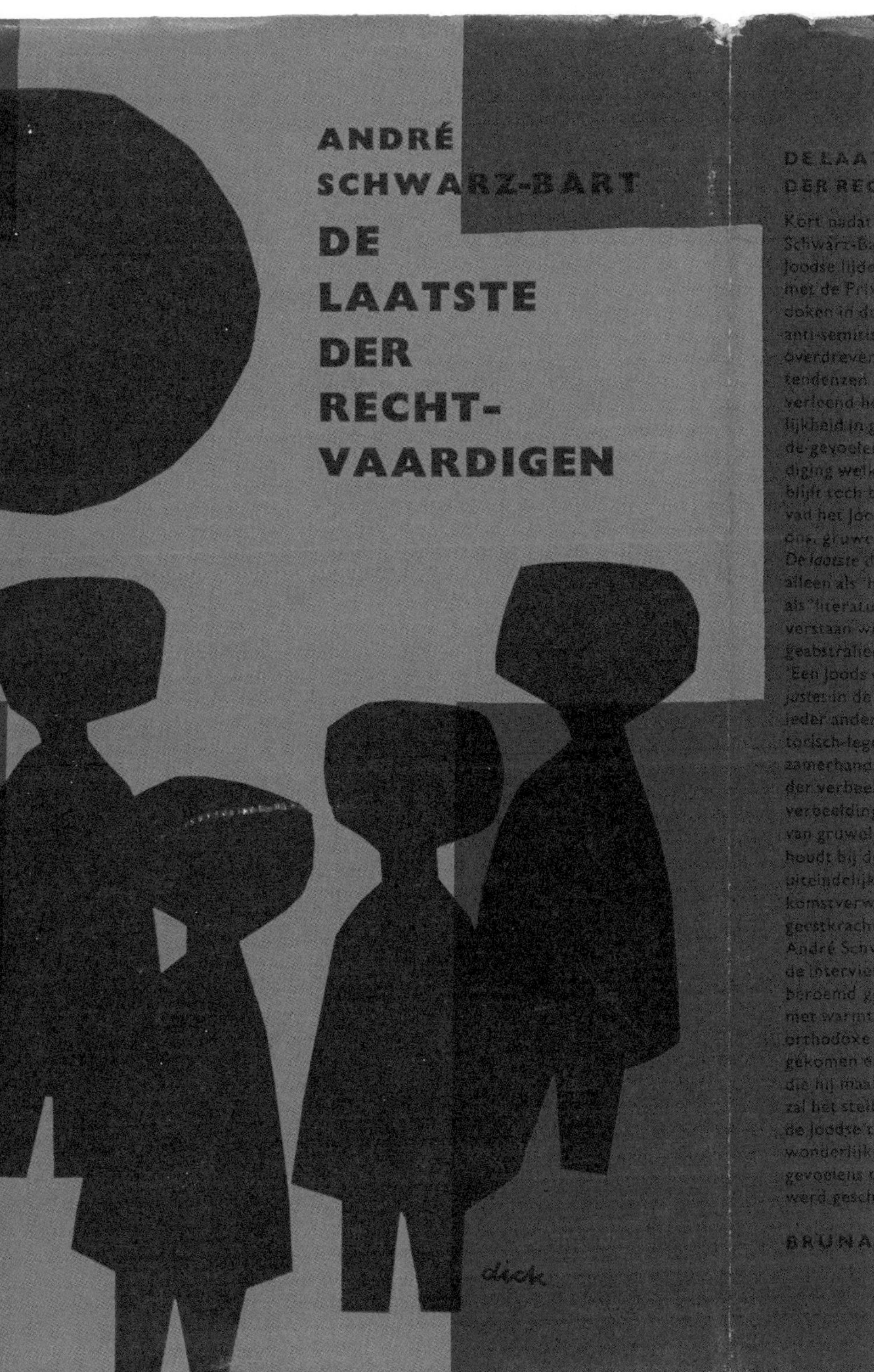

15 Dick Bruna
cover for André Schwarz-Bart,
De laatste der rechtvaardigen
(*The Last of the Just*)
1961

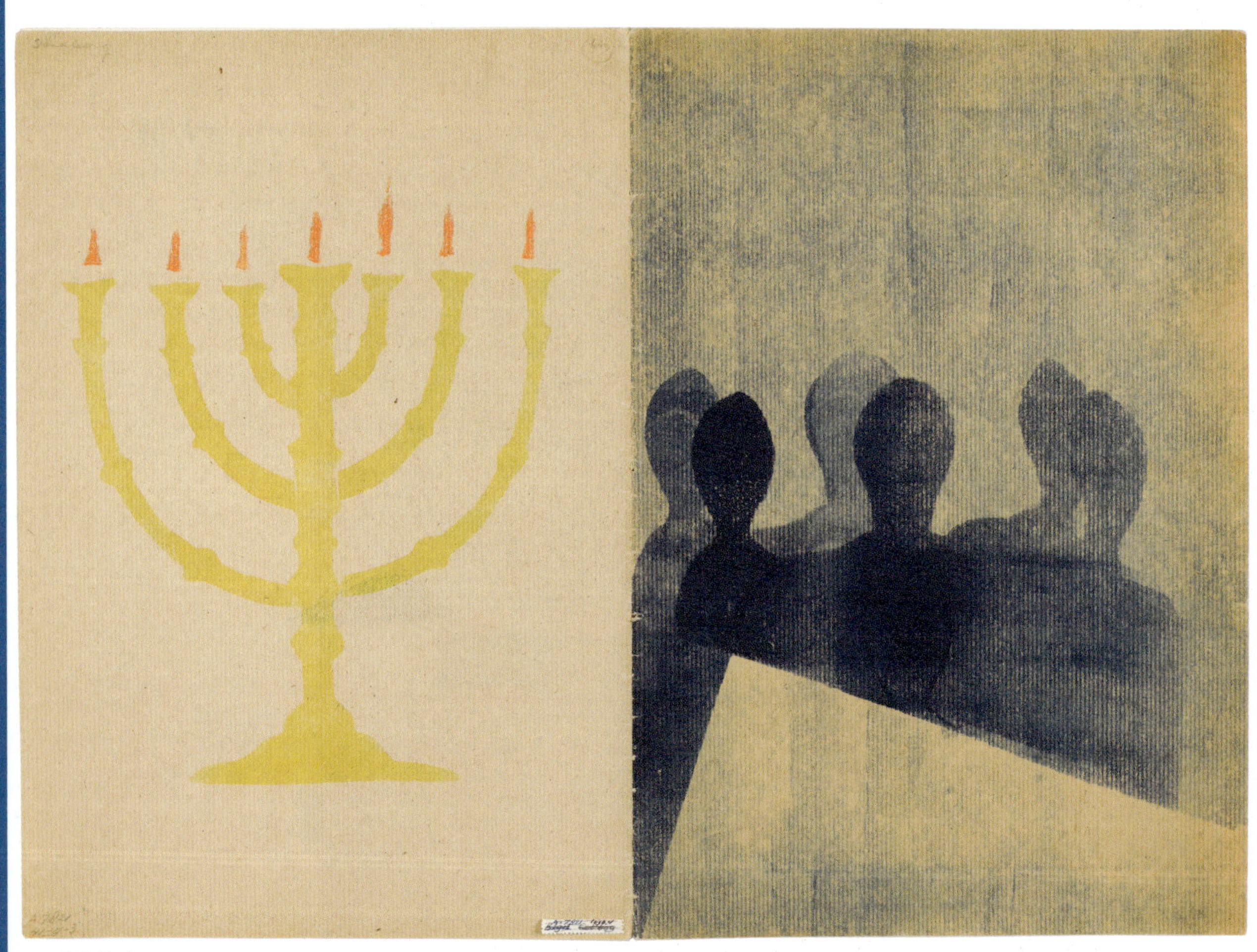

16 H.N. Werkman
Sabbatsgesänge
(*Sabbath Singing*)
1941

DE LAATSTE
DER
RECHTVAARDIGEN

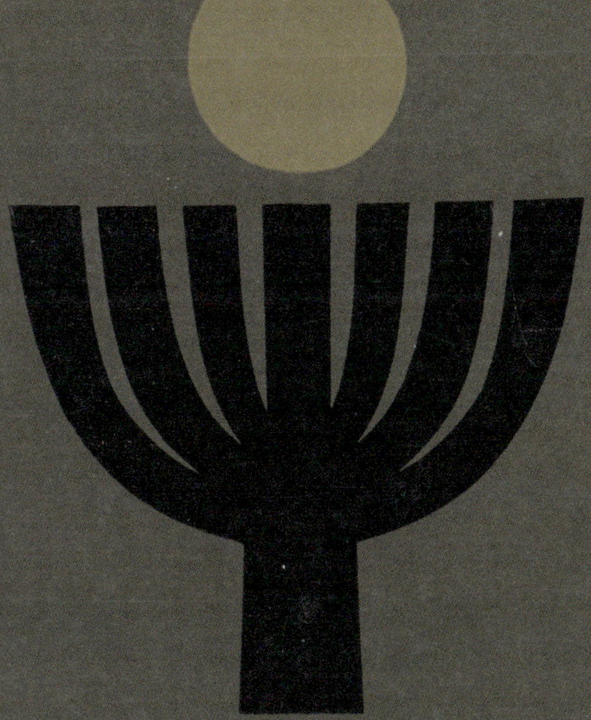

SCHWARZ-BART

dick

17 Dick Bruna
cover for André Schwarz-Bart,
De laatste der rechtvaardigen
(*The Last of the Just*)
1961

Bruna

It is striking that Bruna convincingly quotes stylistic elements while retaining individuality, feeling and atmosphere. Before Bruna began a *Zwarte Beertjes* jacket, he always read the complete manuscript to grasp the essence of the story. When he leafed through a book by Simenon, he immediately imagined himself in Paris:

> 'When I had read three pages,
> I was instantly in Paris in a drizzle
> that could persist for weeks.
> I always tried to get a lot of mist
> on to those jackets, concealing
> much, but not all. A lot of boats
> featured in the Maigret series and
> they often travelled in the dark,
> so I went to the Amsterdam-
> Rhine Canal in the middle of the
> night to get the feel of a boat
> in the dark water.'[7]

On the cover of *Maigret en het lijk zonder hoofd* (*Maigret and the Headless Corpse*) [FIG. 18], the dark silhouettes of the cut-out boats with lighted windows make the sound of ships' horns and the wash against the bows almost audible. The title intensifies the suspense that the image has already suggested.

Art historian Bert Jansen rightly observed that while Bruna makes visual references, his sensitive feeling for form enabled him to convert the signals that he had received in Paris and elsewhere into instantly recognizable, idiosyncratic images.[8] His cover designs were never entirely based on Werkman, Sandberg or Léger, but on a combination of their practices. The new image was original and authentic, and Bruna's personal style remained manifestly consistent. His entire composition, not just his iconic shapes are simple, harmonious, rather compact, and brightly coloured and they avoid discord. Even when suspense was evoked, blood flowed or weapons could be seen, the atmosphere is never ominous. A body is never flesh and blood, but atmospheric and expressive. A murder does not grab us by the throat, but the presence of death is suggested. There is always room for our own reading. That is how you recognize a Bruna.

18 Dick Bruna
cover for Georges Simenon,
Maigret en het lijk zonder hoofd
(*Maigret and the Headless Corpse*)
1968

SIMENON

MAIGRET

dick

en het lijk zonder hoofd

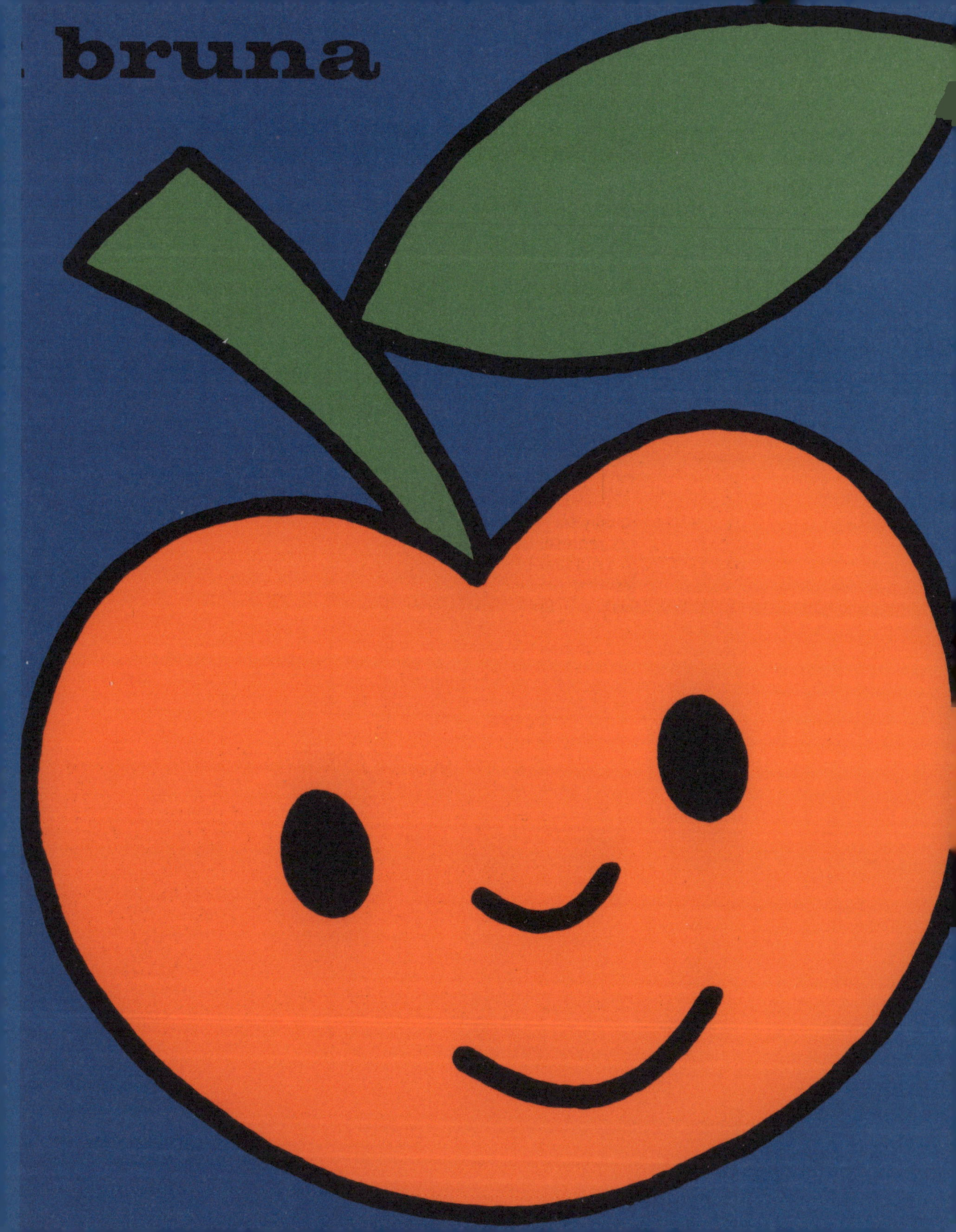
bruna

BRUNA AND MATISSE

The influence of the avant-garde was not confined to the cover art Dick Bruna made for the *Zwarte Beertjes*. Stylistic characteristics of the predecessors and contemporaries he admired are likewise evident in his non-applied work. Bruna's autonomous print *Twee vissen* (*Two Fish*), for example, resonates strongly with a creation by Georges Braque (1882–1963) in the avant-garde magazine *Derrière le Miroir* [FIGS. 19A, B]. Placing two stylized figures inside an ellipse was a favourite device of the Cubist artist. Bruna tore shapes out of paper for his designs, which makes the tribute to Braque and Cubism, a movement that celebrated collage, even clearer.

In most of Bruna's autonomous work, however, we see above all the unmistakable influence of the great master, Matisse. Bruna kept reproductions of works by Matisse in a folder marked 'sources of inspiration'. In one of them we see a lifelike woman's face drawn with clear, dark outlines [FIG. 20B] and in another fruit drawn with a few equally simple lines [FIG. 21B]. Bruna achieved this succinct representation of reality in uninterrupted lines in a number of still lifes created only a couple of years later [FIG. 21A]. The woman's face in *Ann Vickers* [FIG. 20A] leaves Bruna's great admiration in no doubt.

With the exception of these early line drawings, in which Bruna quite clearly translated but closely followed his prototype, Matisse inspired Bruna to create something entirely his own. He gleaned what he saw and admired and distilled it in his own practice.

> 'I was young and soaked up a lot of impressions. Adapted everything and tried everything. You can see in my drawings from that time that I tried to do it just like Léger, or Matisse. I didn't imitate them, but I picked out what I could use.'[9]

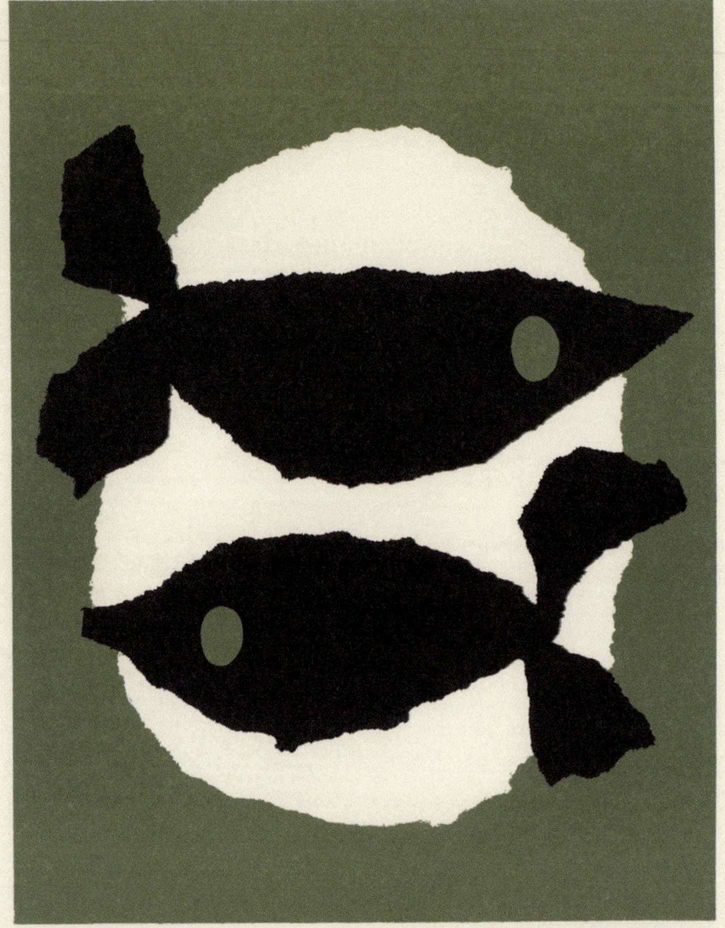

19A
Dick Bruna
Twee vissen
(*Two Fish*)
1962

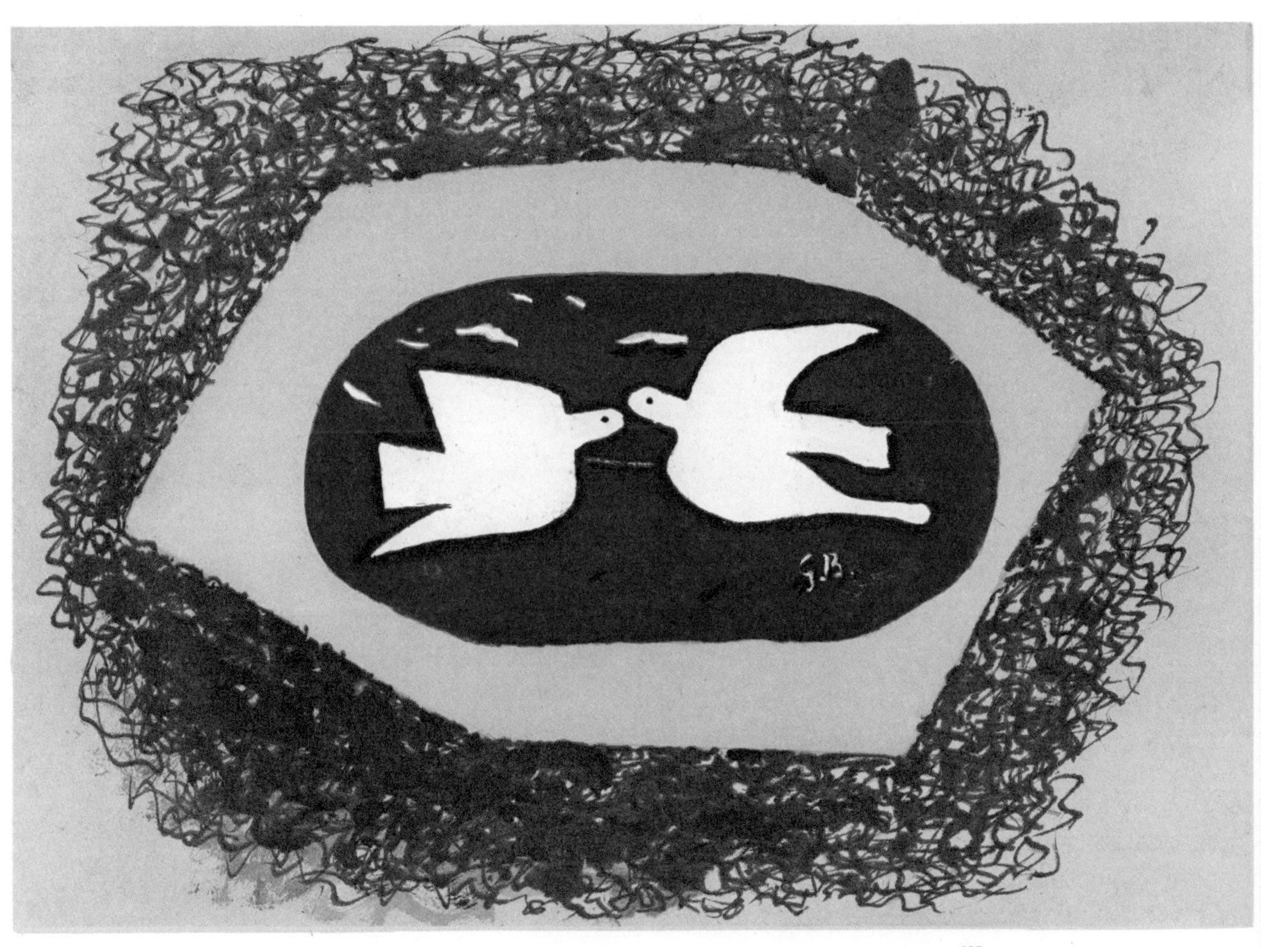

19B
Georges Braque
Deux oiseaux (*Two Birds*),
in the magazine *Derrière le Miroir*
1967

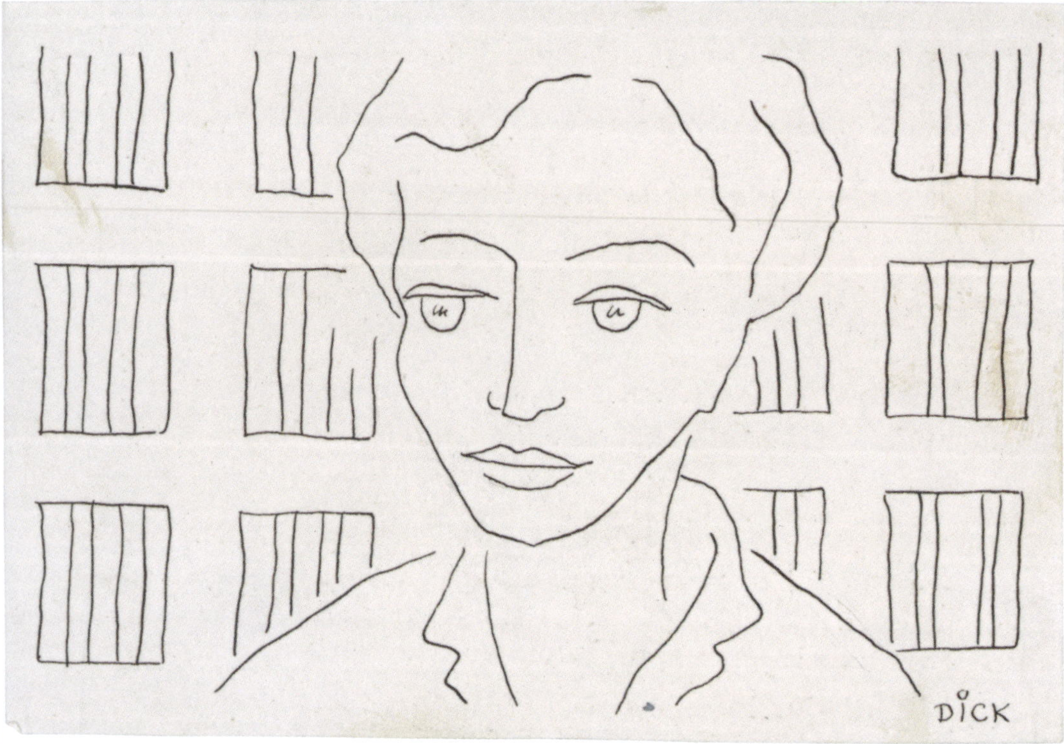

20A
Dick Bruna
cover design for
Sinclair Lewis, *Ann Vickers*
1950–60

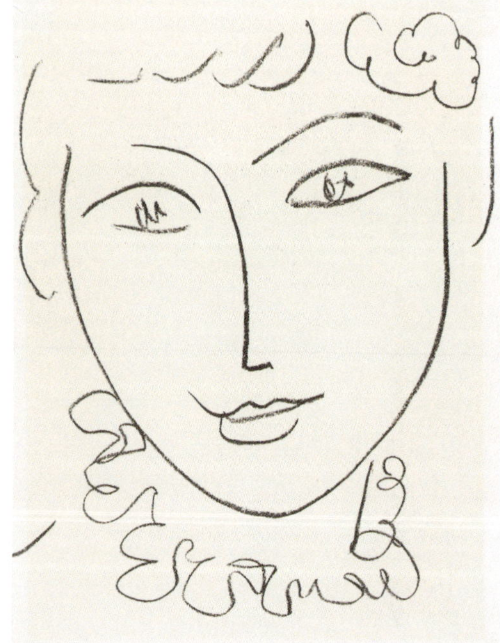

20B
Henri Matisse
La Pompadour,
from the series *Portraits*
in or after 1951–in or before 1954

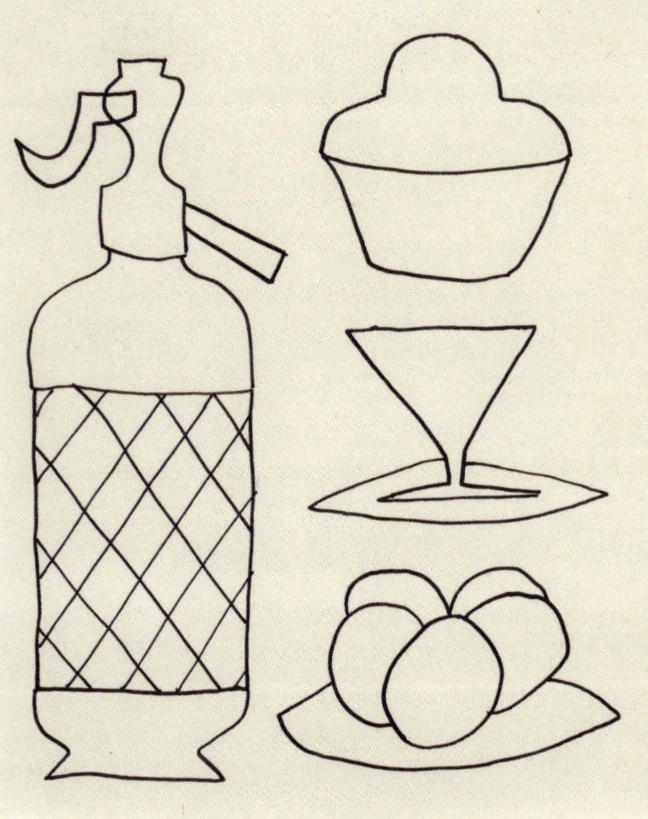

21A
Dick Bruna
Still Life
1953

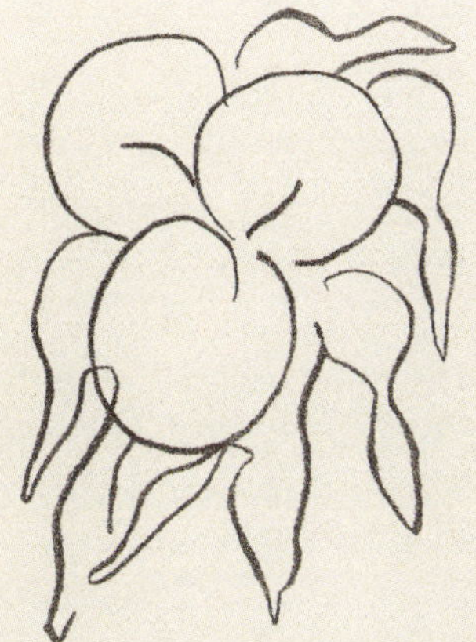

21B
Henri Matisse
Fruits, from the series
Les lithographies de l'Atelier Mourlot, Paris
1946 (design)–1964 (print)

Jazz

In the work *Forms* in the musical artist's book *Jazz* by Matisse, we can see a negative and a positive cut-out, which are slightly different, but clearly related [FIG. 22]. Both the blue and the white torso break away from the background, which nevertheless continues to function as a form in its own right. The abandonment of the third dimension, as in *Jazz* and a large part of Matisse's oeuvre, gave Bruna the freedom he sought:

> 'Just by dropping the traditional perspective, I was immediately able to do everything I wanted. If I didn't need to create space in a drawing, I could do anything, I was unlimited.'[10]

The insight he gained from Matisse – that 'negative forms' could be essential elements within a composition – was also a revelation to the young Bruna: 'I made Miffy because the shape appealed to me: an oval head and two ears. The negative shape that was created is quite beautiful. This means that the background acquires added value: a white shape stands out splendidly against a blue or yellow background. I tended to concentrate on those sorts of problems.'[11] The space between Miffy's ears is just as important as the ears themselves, irrespective of the colour.

In *de appel* (*the apple*) [FIG. 23], Bruna's first autonomous book of prints, what he meant by that becomes clear. The red apple stands out against a green and blue background. The shape of the background, the negative of the apple, is as carefully considered as the centrally placed fruit. This may seem obvious, but it is not.

The print *nijntje in het bos* (*miffy in the forest*) [FIG. 24] is just as exciting, if not more so; it was based on a page from the book *nijntje op de fiets* (*miffy's bicycle*). The negative forms in this composition are created by the white cut-aways between two rows of trees. But at first glance it is not the green of the trunks that you grasp, but the vacuum, as if there were objects in the foreground. This has to do with the inherent properties of the non-colour white, and with the visual rhyme between the pointed shapes, like the outline of Gothic windows, and Miffy's only visible ear. The positive shape of the ear is repeated no fewer than five times within the negative forms. It is only the knowledge that the trees are in the foreground that makes the eye zoom in again. Because of this, our eyes and brain find themselves in conflict, and foreground and background continually seem to shift. In combination with the repetition of shapes, this shifting focus creates a musical, *jazz*-like rhythm.

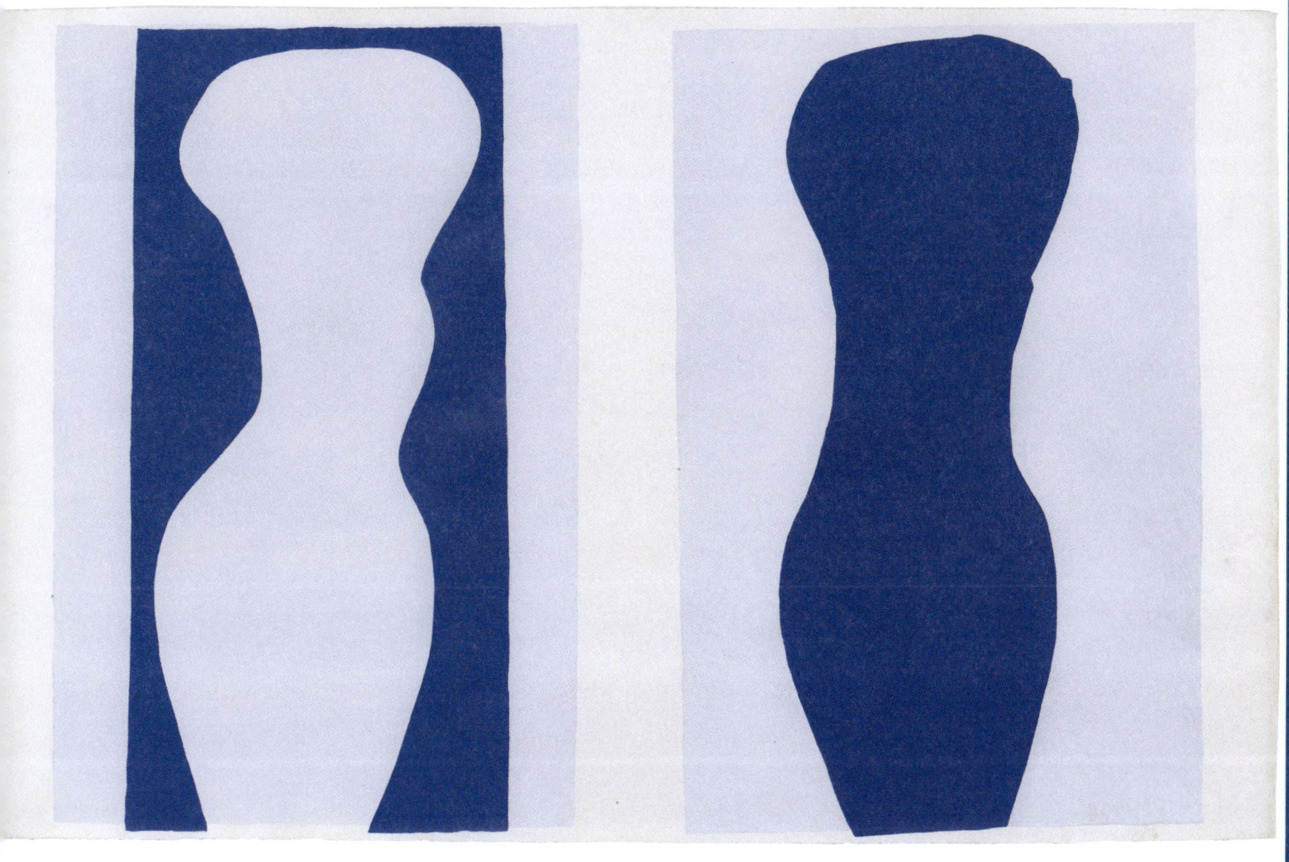

22 Henri Matisse
Jazz no. 9, Forms, pages in the artist's book *Jazz*
1947

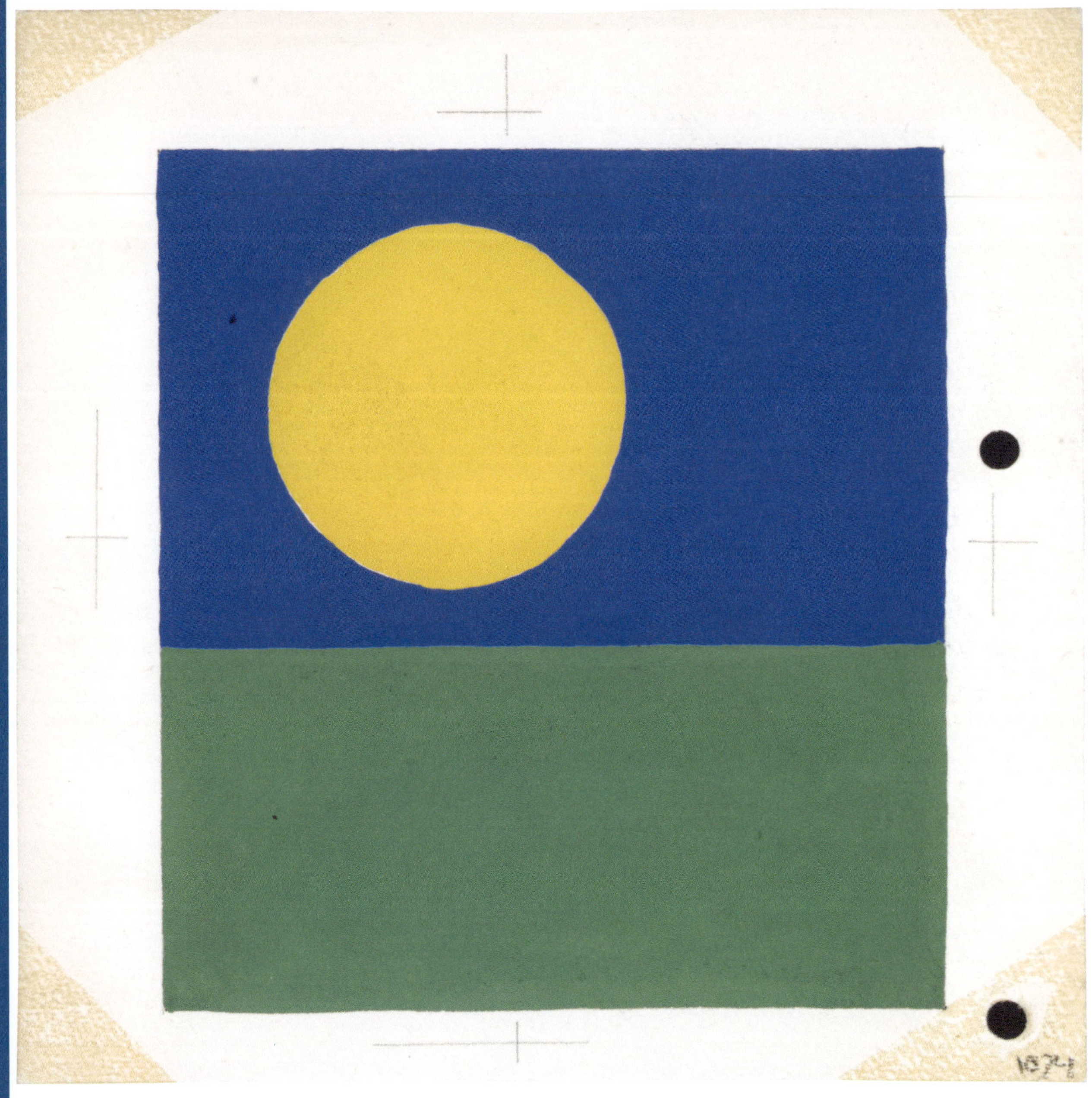

23 Dick Bruna
designs for *de appel*
(*the apple*)
1953

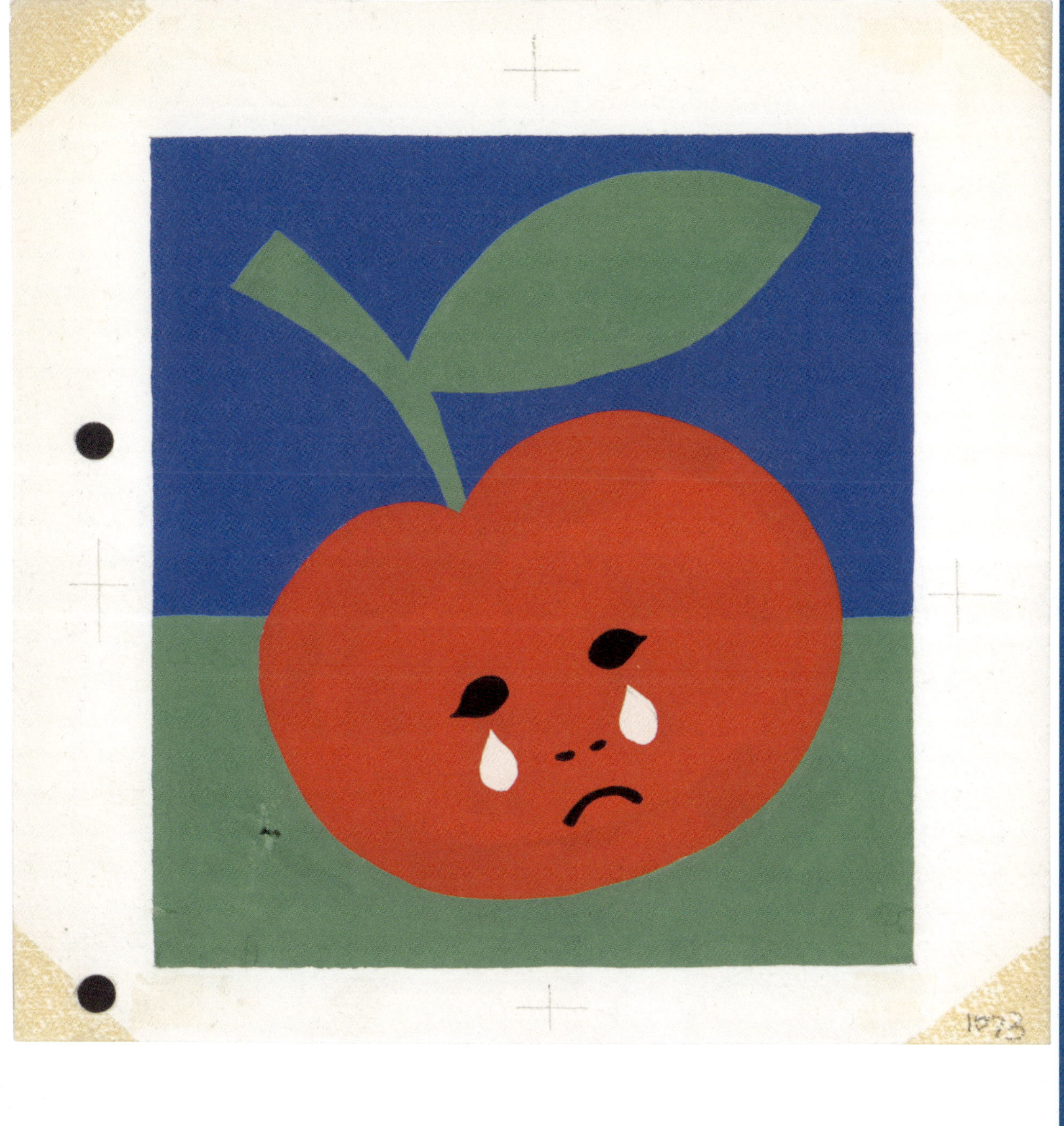

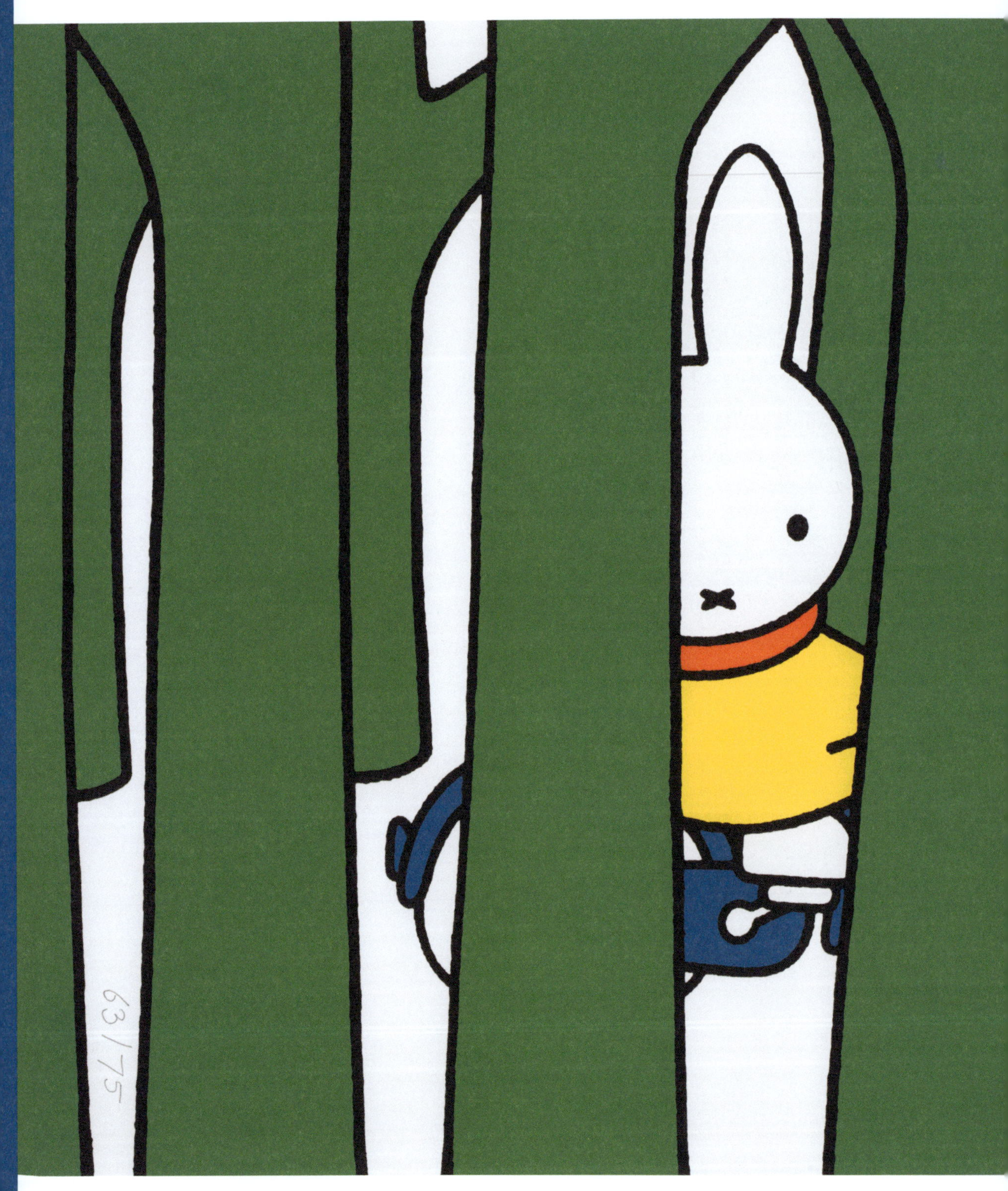
63/75

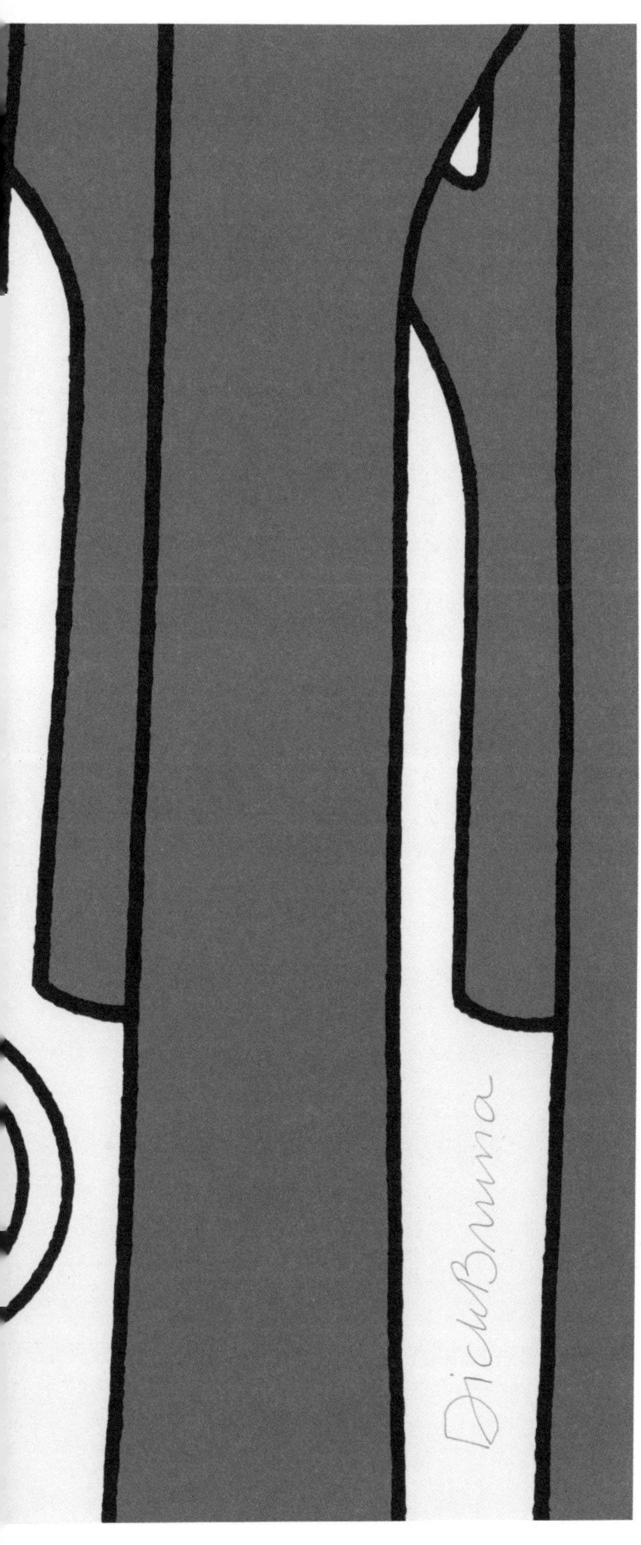

24 Dick Bruna
nijntje in het bos
(*miffy in the forest*)
2007

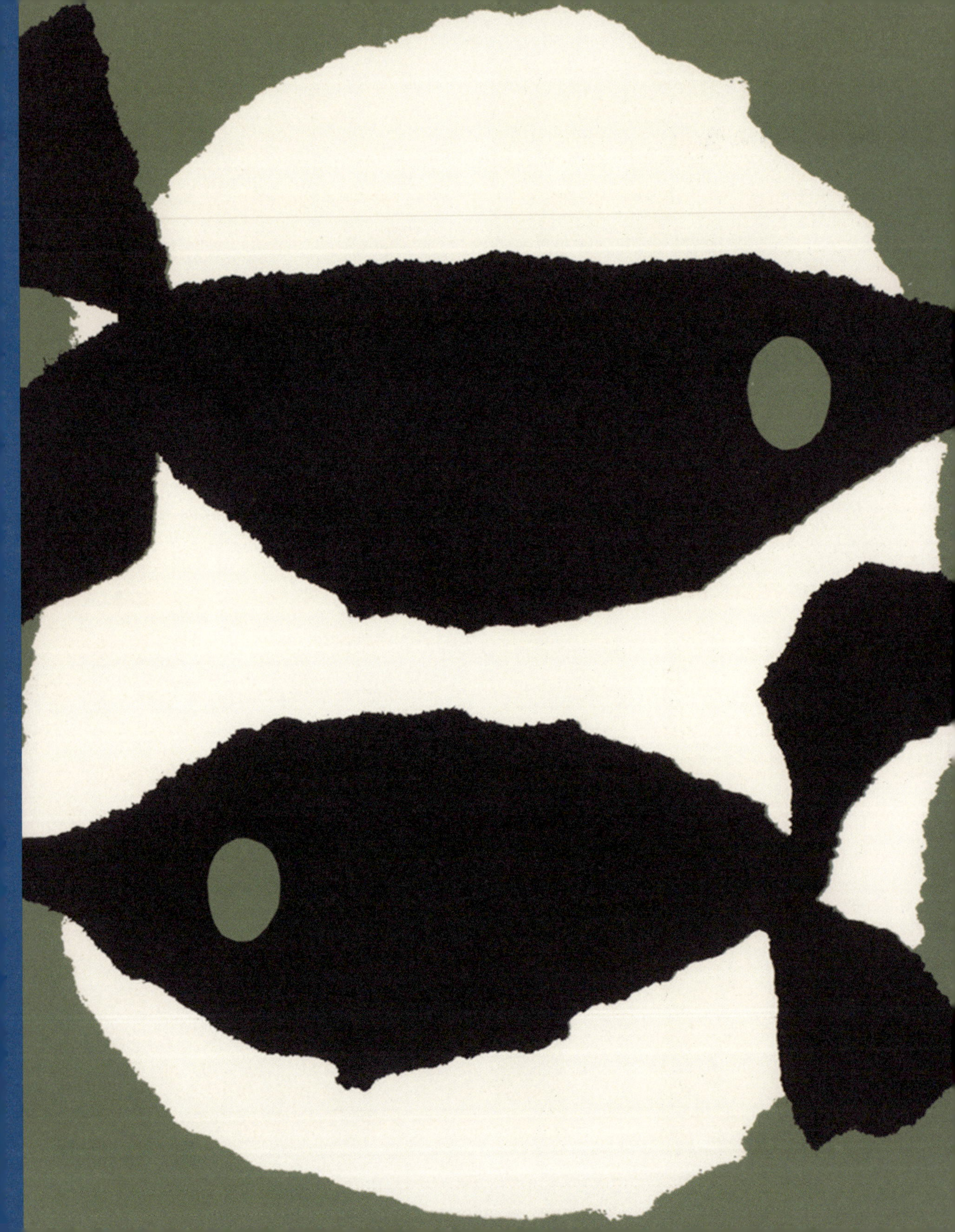

Chapelle du Rosaire

An obvious difference between Bruna's and Matisse's cut-outs is the black outlines. A couple of years after the first publication of *de appel* (*the apple*), Bruna added outlines to the figures in this book [FIGS. 25A, B]. It was a very successful move, and the book became more popular. These 'quivering' lines, as he calls them, which have such a powerful visual impact, were to become a regular feature of his work. In only a few exceptional cases, like *de koning* (*the king*; 1955), are the figures not outlined. According to Bruna, the inspiration for the lines came from Fernand Léger, and from a chapel in Vence decorated by Matisse. Matisse designed the windows, the altar and the murals for the Chapelle du Rosaire between 1948 and 1951. He used scissors to create the design for the stained glass [FIG. 26]. Although he was satisfied with the result, he had given no thought to the lead that would be required. The metal needed to hold the pieces of coloured glass inevitably created dark dividing lines, so Matisse made a second design in which he incorporated the lead lines into the composition [FIG. 27].

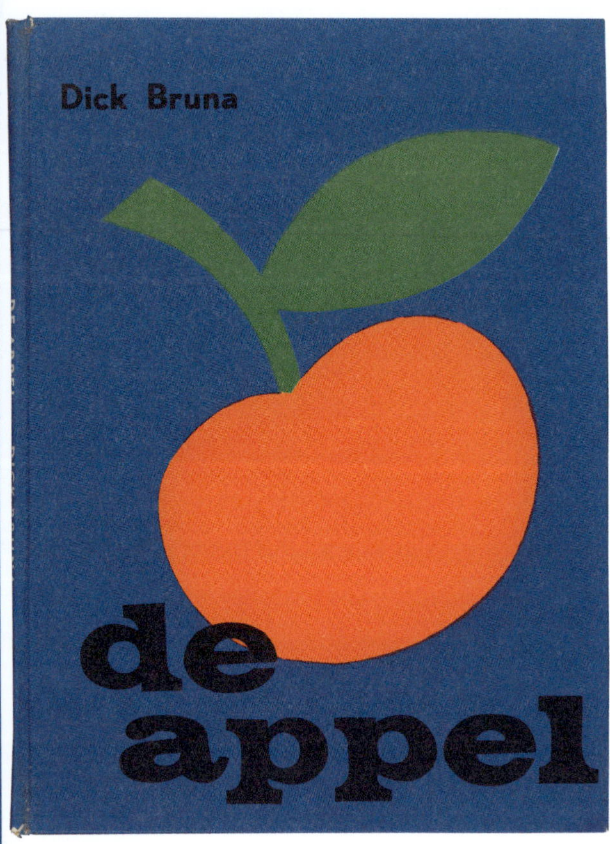

25A
Dick Bruna
cover of *de appel*
(*the apple*)
1953 (first edition)

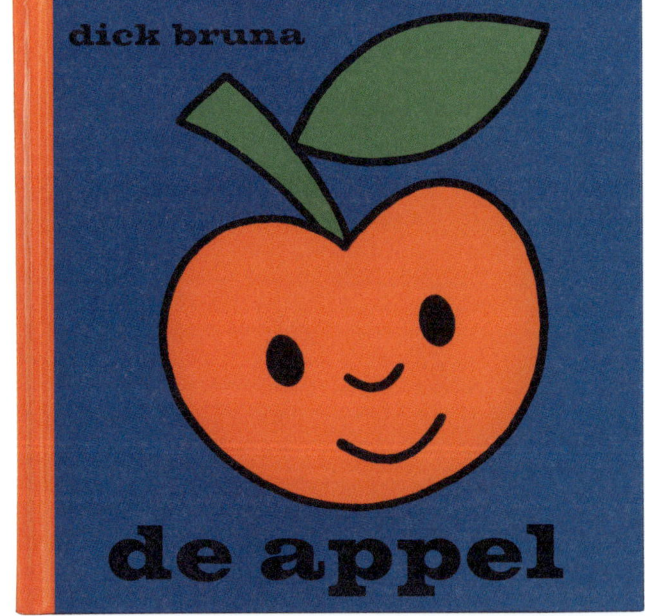

25B
Dick Bruna
cover of *de appel*
(*the apple*)
1959

26 Henri Matisse
design for stained-glass window for the Chapelle du Rosaire in Vence
1951

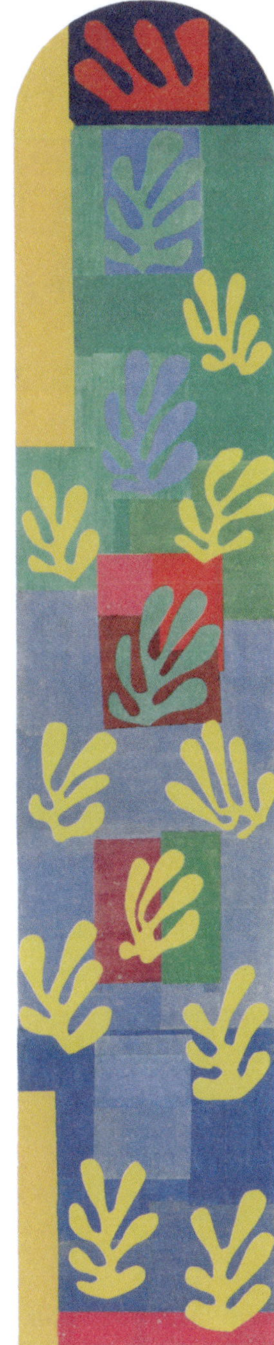

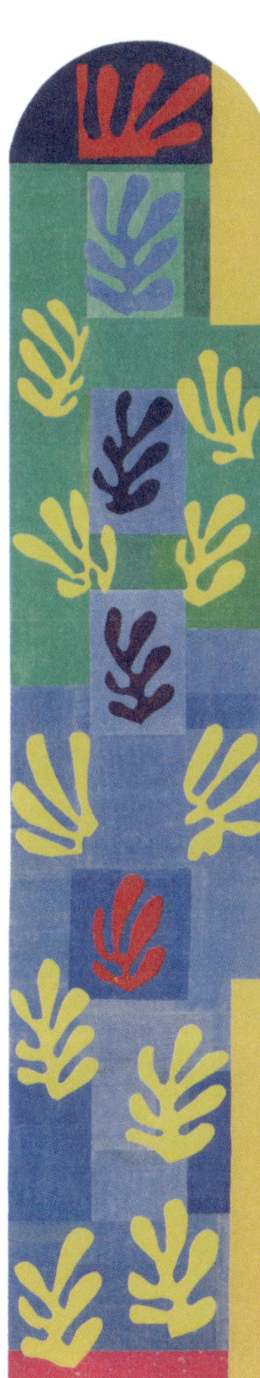

27 Henri Matisse
detail of second design for stained-glass window for the Chapelle du Rosaire in Vence
1951

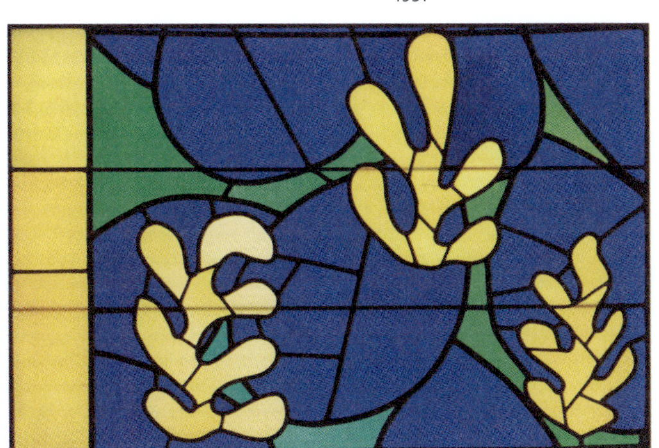

The Sheaf

Bruna made a more anecdotal reference to Matisse in *nijntje in het museum* (*miffy at the gallery*):

> that one is fine, said miffy
> the colours are so clear
> as if the artist cut them out
> and stuck them on up there

Like Matisse, Bruna cut out his shapes directly from solid coloured paper. The almost exaggerated traces of the scissors can even be seen from a distance in the rabbits' heads on the wall of the imaginary white cube gallery [FIG. 29]. 'I still see the collages [by Matisse] before me. That clarity, that simplicity, I was very moved by them. I thought then that this was fantastic, to be able to tell something with such limited means. I immediately thought that this is my world. It was recognition.'[12]

Matisse's individual cut-outs, such as a Fatsia leaf, often consisted of minuscule and larger pieces of paper stuck on top of one another, although the streamlined outline suggested otherwise. Matisse endeavoured to define his shapes exactly to the millimetre, driving his assistants mad by making them add a square so tiny as to be almost invisible. The supposed spontaneity that we associate with his work was often, in fact, highly calculated. Bruna's cut-outs, by contrast, are always a single piece of paper, but, like Matisse's, they are very carefully considered.

The work Miffy admires in the nameless museum found its origin in *The Sheaf* by Matisse [FIG. 28]. The 'fingers' of the leaves were cleverly converted by Bruna into rabbits' ears. Something instantly strikes you: the characteristic outlines are lacking. Because Bruna rarely used perspective or shadow effects, the dark fringes are an ideal means of ensuring that the figures do not merge into the surrounding space. But in this case they are absent. The little coloured heads consequently suggest tissue-thin pieces of paper attached directly to the wall, like *The Sheaf*. Had they had the customary black outline, they would have seemed to float in front of the wall. This is clearly a homage, so Bruna translated it as literally as possible.

A tiny detail reveals that the cut-outs are probably not portraits of just any rabbit. Miffy's right ear in *miffy at the gallery* is larger than her left: most of the rabbits' heads on the wall also appear to have a slightly longer ear on the same side.

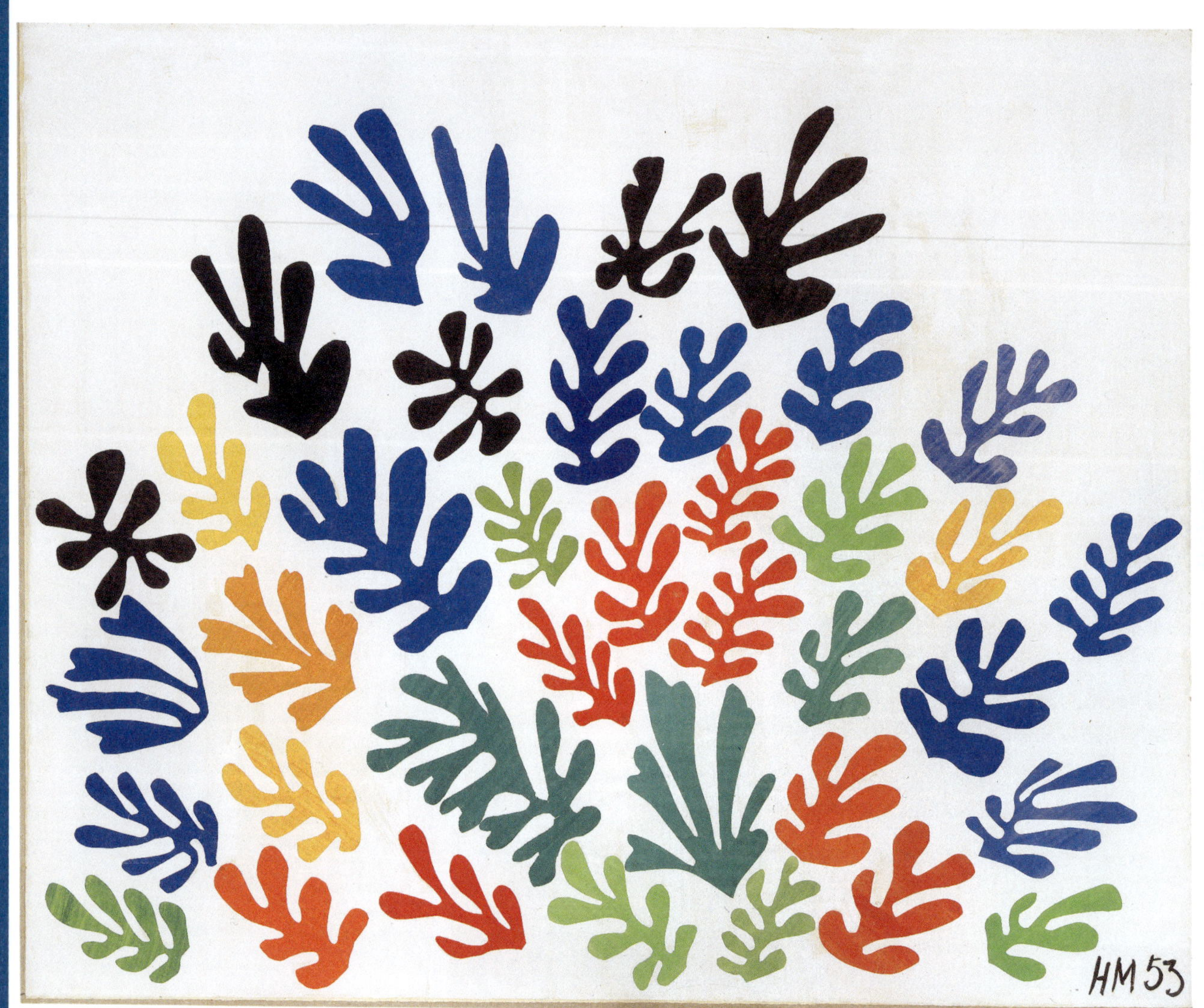

28 Henri Matisse
The Sheaf
1953

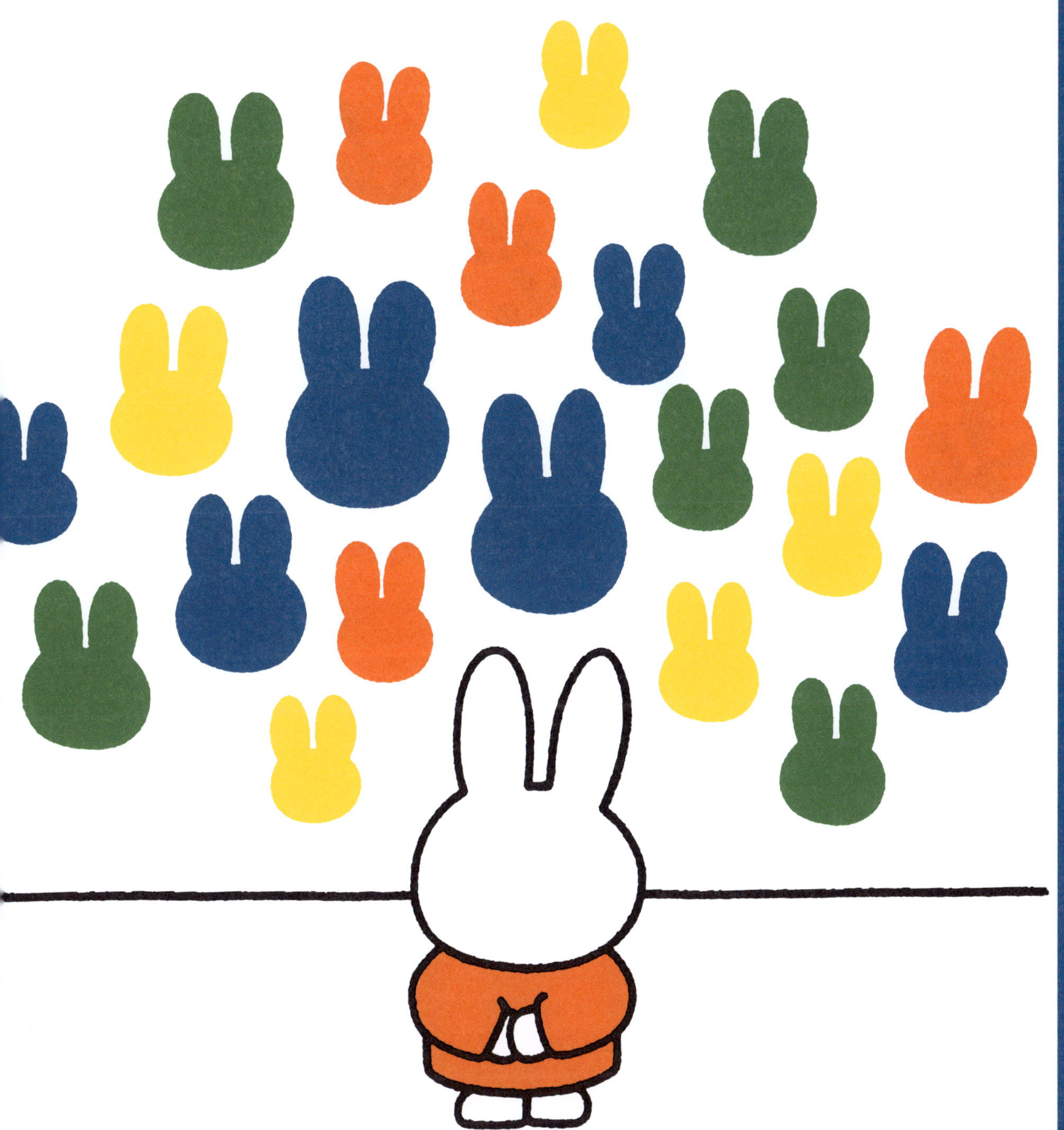

29 Dick Bruna
Miffy and Matisse,
in *nijntje in het museum*
(*miffy at the gallery*)
1997

BRUNA AND DE STIJL

'Young man – that is a really beautiful little shape.' Bruna spent a year with his head in the clouds after this remark by Gerrit Rietveld, one of the prominent figures in De Stijl. The meeting took place at the time when, as a young designer, Dick was working on the cover for *De Saint wordt piraat* (*The Pirate Saint*) and Rietveld attended a meeting about a book that A.W. Bruna & Zn. was going to publish for him. The compliment related to an oval halo [FIG. 30]: a fairly unusual shape for Rietveld.

The general characteristics of De Stijl, the famous and highly influential Dutch art movement (active 1917–31), were a radical degree of simplification or abstraction of forms, straight black lines that enclosed uniform planes, coloured or not, and a palette reduced to primary colours with the addition of black, white and grey. The key exponents, Piet Mondrian (1872–1944), Theo van Doesburg (1883–1931) and Gerrit Rietveld (1888–1964), saw these pure colours and the non-colours white, black and grey as objective, universal and normative – although some, like the independent-minded Van Doesburg, often chose to ignore this.

30 Dick Bruna
cover for Leslie Charteris,
De Saint wordt piraat
(*The Pirate Saint*)
1961

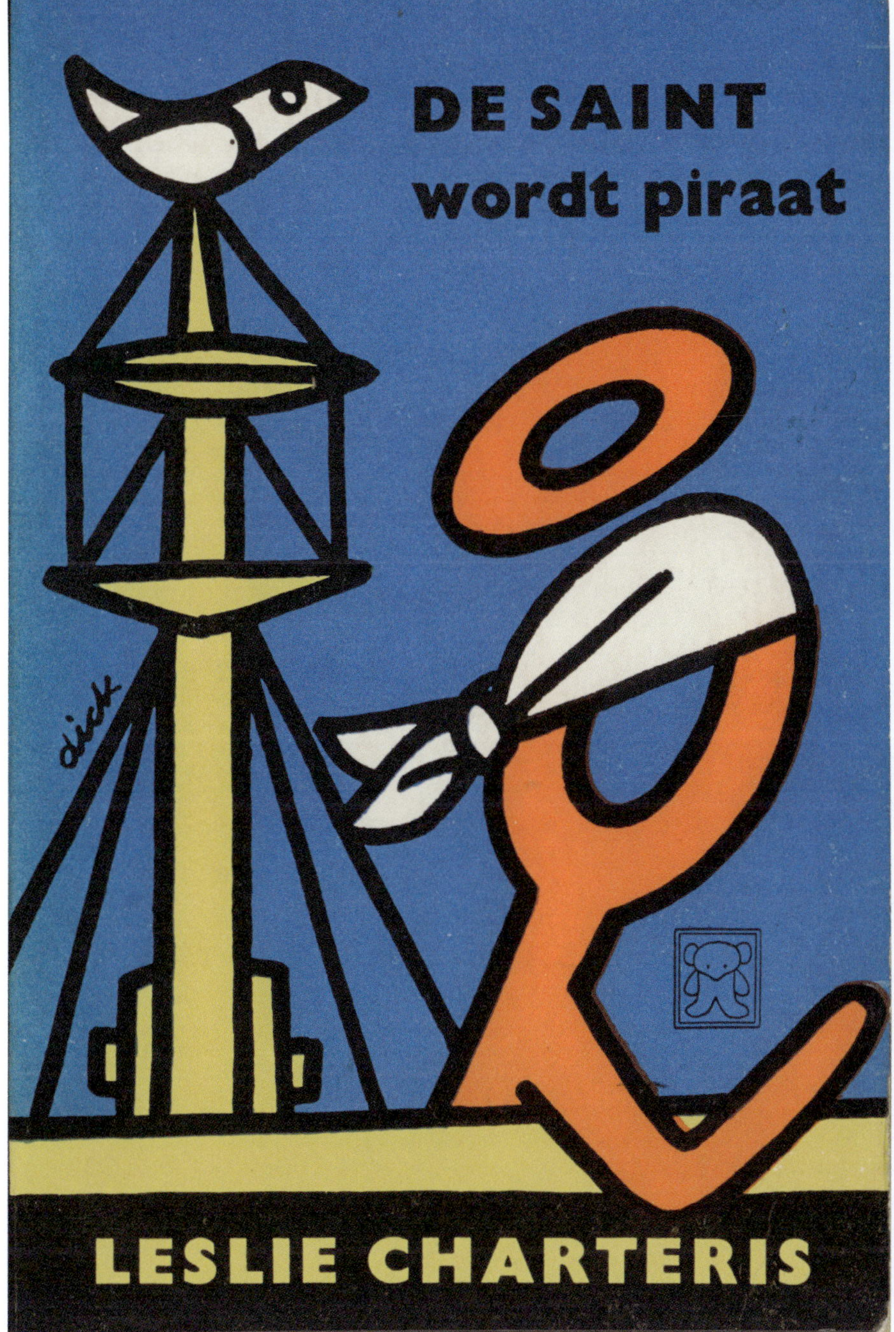

Van der Leck

Bruna was greatly inspired by the work of a number of members of De Stijl, though others met with less approval. He thought Mondrian was too abstract and began to appreciate him only later in life. It was precisely for that reason that the early work of Bart van der Leck (1876–1958) appealed to him. 'Van der Leck has been the most important member of the De Stijl group for me. He started from reality and tried to reduce it to the most essential.'[13] It was not until the 1950s, when Van der Leck had already disassociated himself from De Stijl, that his work became purely abstract. Before that, the compositions he painted were usually figurative.

Van der Leck built up his compositions from coloured, geometric fields against a white background. The lack of lines and the white space between the coloured areas created a figurative space for the free association of the viewer. It is the viewer who 'completes' the image, which does not actually exist, by drawing imaginary lines. Van der Leck called an image hidden in a composition 'the latent'. This concept underpins the success of Bruna's designs. The viewer has the opportunity to project his own ideas, images and details. Bruna's creations, such as the *Zwarte Beertjes* protagonists the Saint and the Shadow, and Miffy too, have only iconic properties and lack the specific.

From 1963 onwards, a design for a picture in the Miffy series has always consisted of a collage and a separate transparent film with black lines that together form the end result. If the collage is looked at without the film overlay and hence with no outlines [FIG. 31], the communality of Bruna and Van der Leck becomes even more obvious. At first glance the coloured geometric planes surrounded by white space come across as abstract. Because the relationship between the shapes does suggest lines, however, after some effort the actual composition appears in the mind's eye, like *Composition* (*Milkmaid with a Cow*) by Van der Leck, where it is the title that directs the eye [FIG. 32].

Although they both emphasized the two-dimensionality of their medium and took the reduction and abstraction of recognizable reality to the extreme, there are also manifest differences between Van der Leck and Bruna. For example *Composition* (*Milkmaid with a Cow*) is made up of countless fragmented planes and there is even a hint of detail: the cow's hoofs, the dress in blue and white, the red headdress and the hand with the halter. A Miffy print is much simpler, just a few uniformly coloured, black-outlined planes that often continue to the edge of the image. In that sense, despite the role of figuration, there appears to be a greater stylistic affinity to Mondrian, who also bordered coloured fields with black lines in his iconic works.

31 Dick Bruna
cover design for *de brief van nijntje* (*miffy's letter*)
2003

Compare with fig. 41 on p. 69 where the film is in place

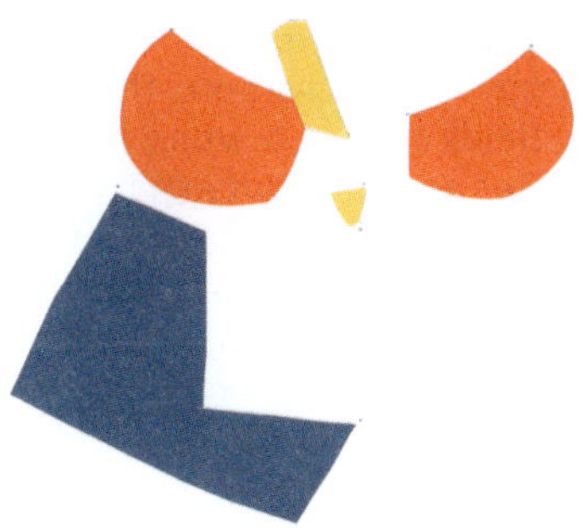

32 Bart van der Leck
Composition (Milkmaid with a Cow)
c. 1921

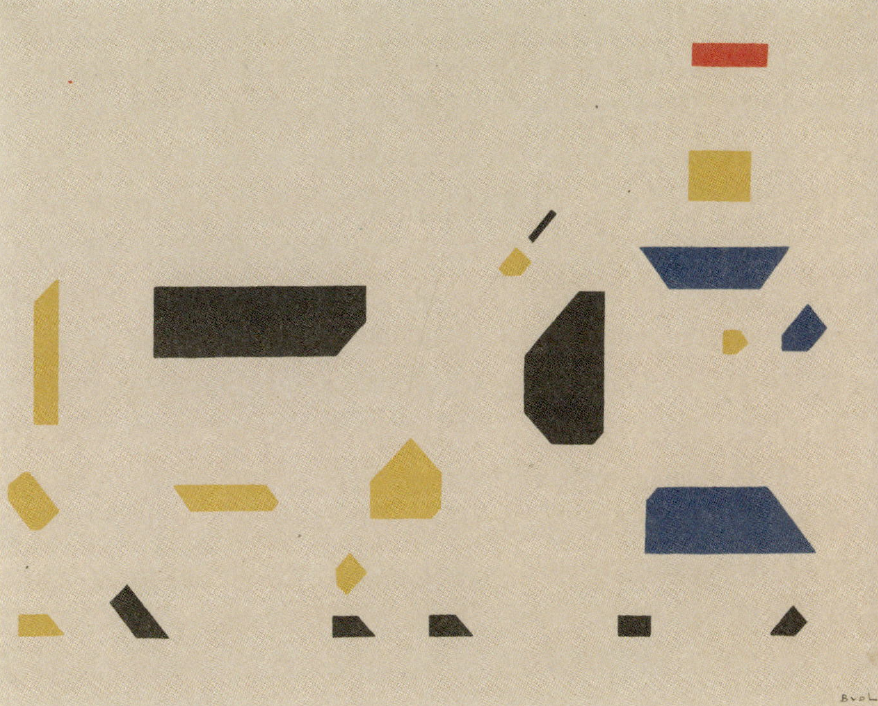

Rietveld

Dick Bruna adopted De Stijl's standardized colours for his own palette, but used slightly different tones. 'They're called the primary colours, but that's not right. Rietveld used the same colours as I do, but his blue is completely different from my blue, and we both think *our* blue is the ultimate blue.'[14] Bruna's red, which he sought for a long time and has remained unchanged for more than fifty years, tends somewhat towards orange. And although he quite often used green, which Mondrian hated, in his book covers, posters and books of prints, he sees it as a compromise, 'I have always tried to confine myself to the primaries, De Stijl colours.'[15] De Stijl did not tolerate the 'spectrum' or 'secondary' colours. Mondrian maintained that these colours expressed 'the old harmony' and were not to be used under any circumstances. Bruna's rules are consequently black for the lines, blue for the sky, green for the grass, yellow for the sun and red for everything else.

Bruna shared more than his palette with De Stijl; the shape of his book of prints also pays tribute to that school – above all to the designer and architect Gerrit Rietveld. In the reissue of *de appel* (*the apple*), the book undergoes a transformation – from rectangular to square [SEE FIGS. 25A, B ON P. 48]. Rietveld had taken the square as his point of departure in his furniture and his architecture. He arranged his designs, such as his famous chairs, in grids, a square forming the base [FIG. 33A]. Very occasionally even a circle appears in a piece of furniture [FIG. 33B]. But regardless of the geometric shape inspired by Rietveld, a square book is a very economical way of using paper. In 1959 Pieter Brattinga, a graphic designer employed by Steendrukkerij De Jong en Co. and at that time Bruna's friend, folded the sheet for a Miffy book so that it produced twenty-four square pages. That meant space for twelve illustrations and twelve accompanying verses, each measuring 15.5 x 15.5 centimetres. Bruna immediately liked the shape because of the association with Rietveld's work – and it also proved to fit easily into small children's hands. The format has remained the same ever since.

The experimental, identically sized *Kwadraatbladen* (*Square Pages*) series, which De Jong en Co. developed between 1955 and 1974, is celebrated for the same unusual shape. Prominent artists and designers, including Marc Chagall and Willem Sandberg [FIG. 34], were asked to produce a *Square Pages* book. The shape of the Miffy books and the 1966 Sandberg publication emanated from the same maker [FIG. 35].[16]

33A
Gerrit Rietveld
Armchair for Til Brugman
c. 1919 (design)–1923 (execution)

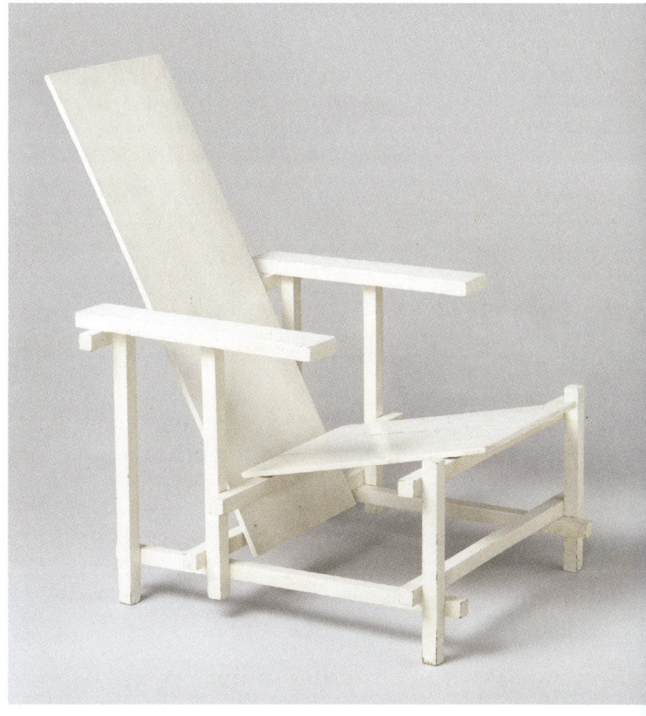

33B
Gerrit Rietveld
Side Table for Til Brugman
1923

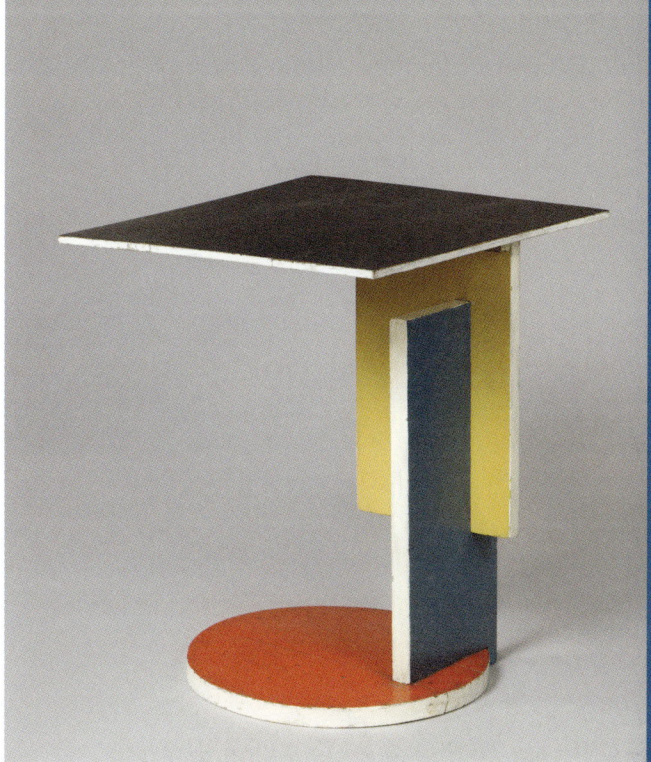

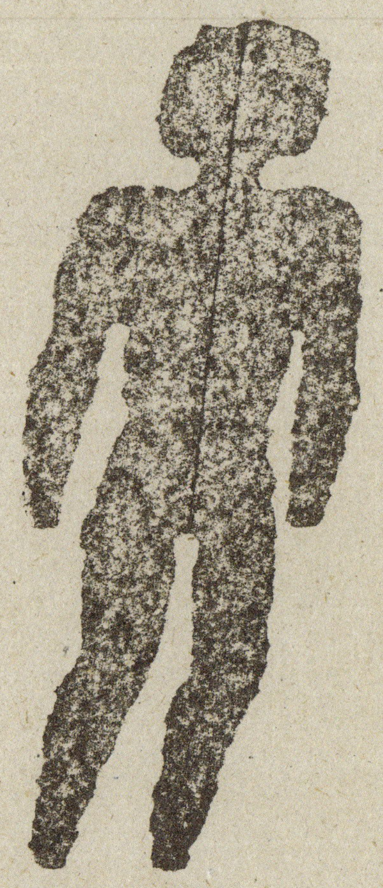

34 Willem Sandberg
Kwadraat-blad
(*Square Page*)
1966

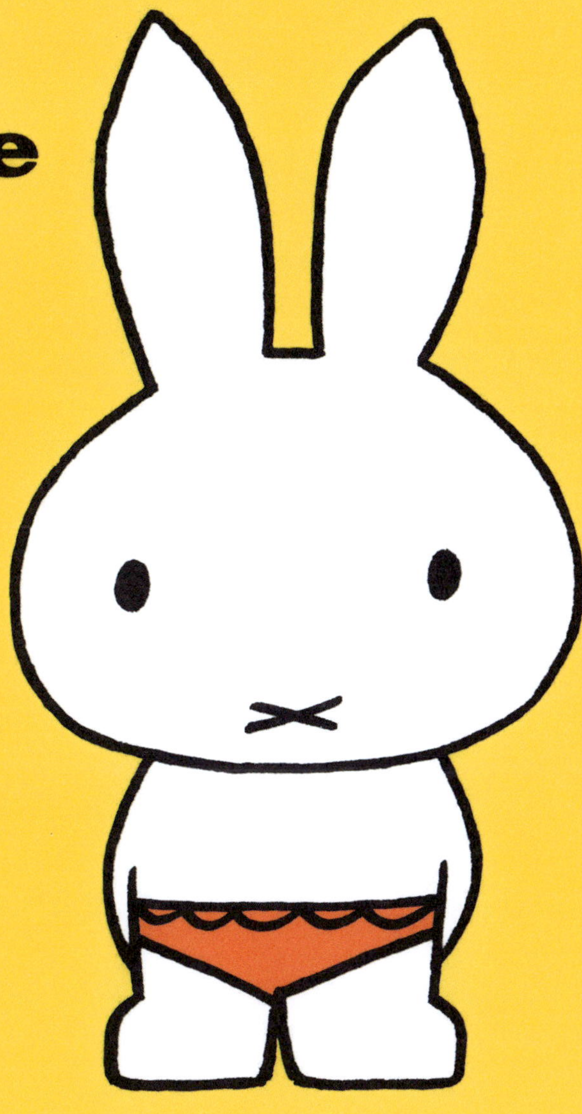

35 Dick Bruna
cover of *nijntje aan zee*
(*miffy at the seaside*)
1996

Van Doesburg and Mondrian

In one of the plates in *nijntje in het museum* (*miffy at the gallery*), Bruna suggests that Miffy is looking at a painting by Van Doesburg or Mondrian [FIGS. 36A, B]. To achieve this, he used primary colours, solid planes of colour and black lines at right angles to each other against a white background within a square frame. But is he quoting an existing painting? The direction of the lines clinches it: although the double lines and the complicated grid refer to the later Mondrian, he kept strictly to the horizontal and the vertical [FIG. 37]. Bruna seems to make a sly joke at the expense of Van Doesburg and Mondrian, who fell out over the diagonal line.[17] In 1924 Theo van Doesburg introduced the *Contra-Compositions*, where the lines were turned forty-five degrees in relation to the support [FIG. 38] to create tension between the lines of the canvas and the composition. Mondrian solved this by standing the canvas on its point so that only the edges of the canvas form diagonals. The debate finally led to the break between Mondrian and Van Doesburg. In a single, playful image, Bruna succeeded in capturing the essence of a major art-historical event. The reference, however, is intuitive. Decades after the quarrel, Bruna unintentionally reconciled two contested visions.

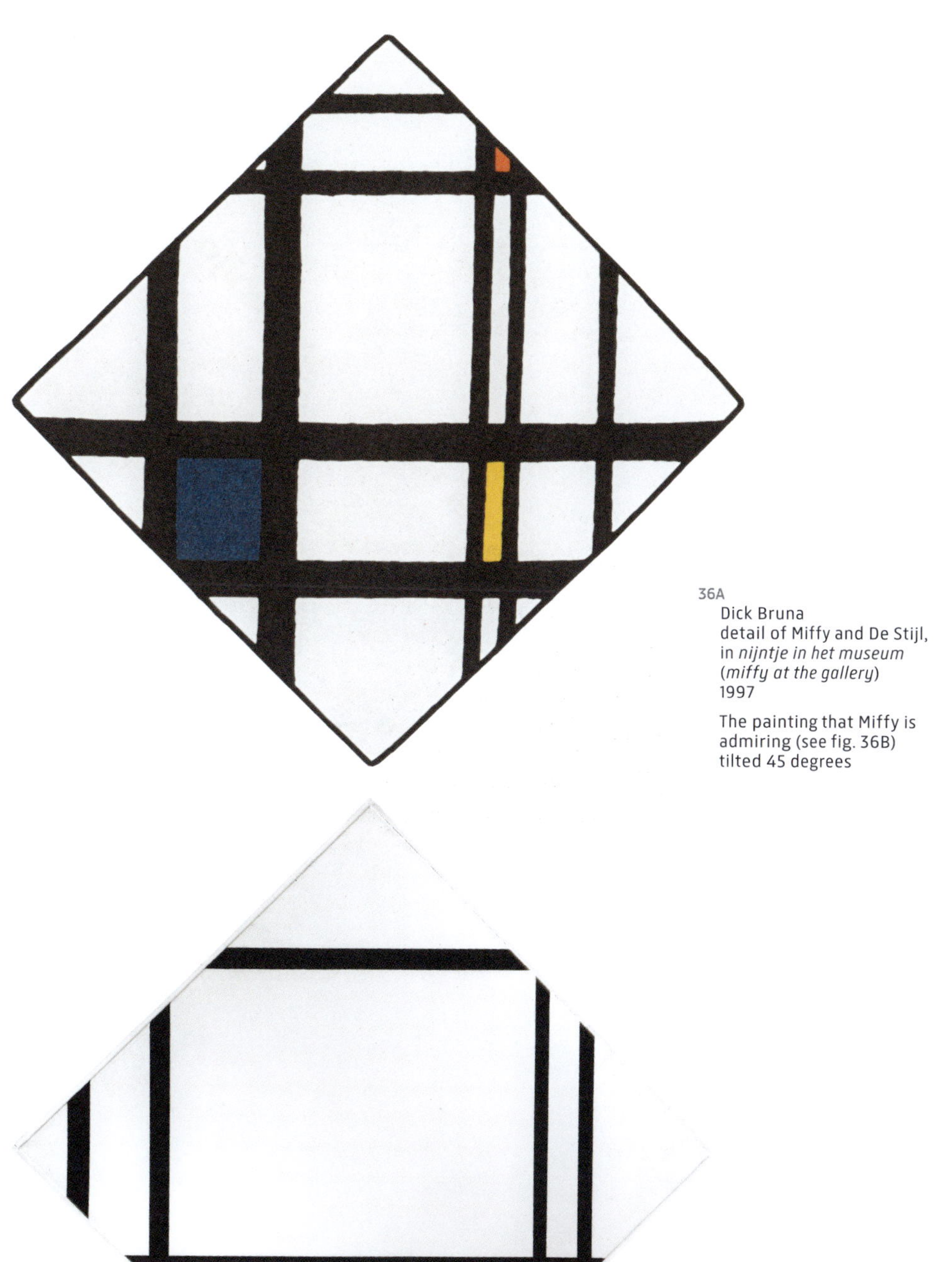

36A
Dick Bruna
detail of Miffy and De Stijl,
in *nijntje in het museum*
(*miffy at the gallery*)
1997

The painting that Miffy is
admiring (see fig. 36B)
tilted 45 degrees

37 Piet Mondrian
Picture No. III; Lozenge Composition with Eight Lines and Red
1938

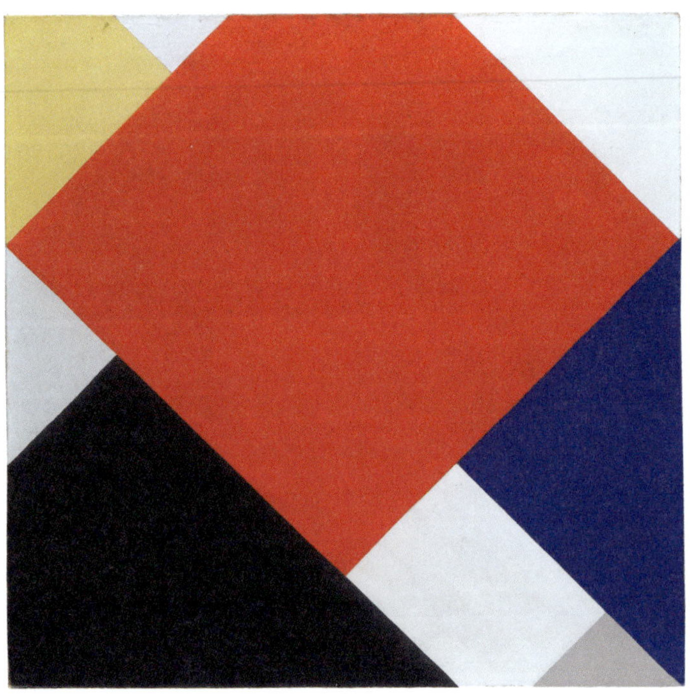

38 Theo van Doesburg
Contra-composition V
1924

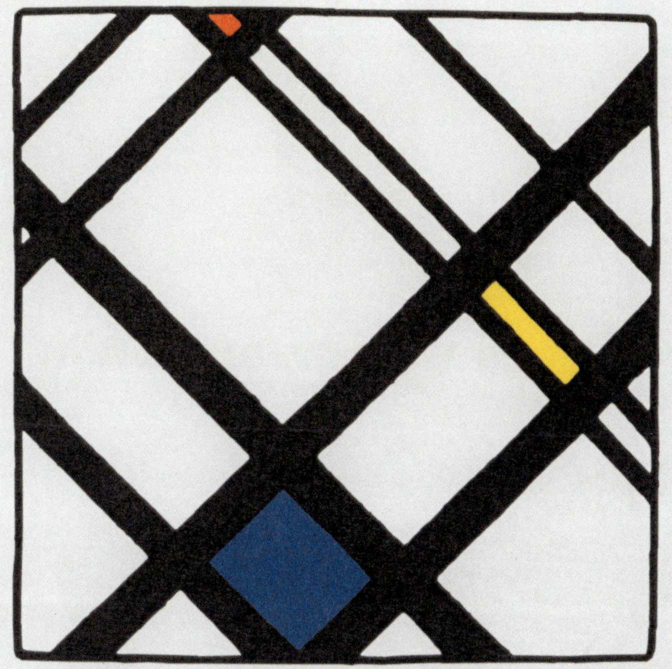

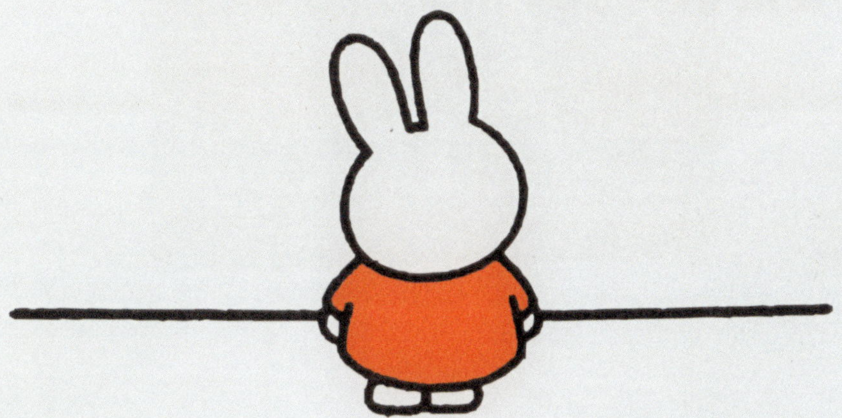

36B
Dick Bruna
Miffy and De Stijl,
in *nijntje in het museum*
(*miffy at the gallery*)
1997

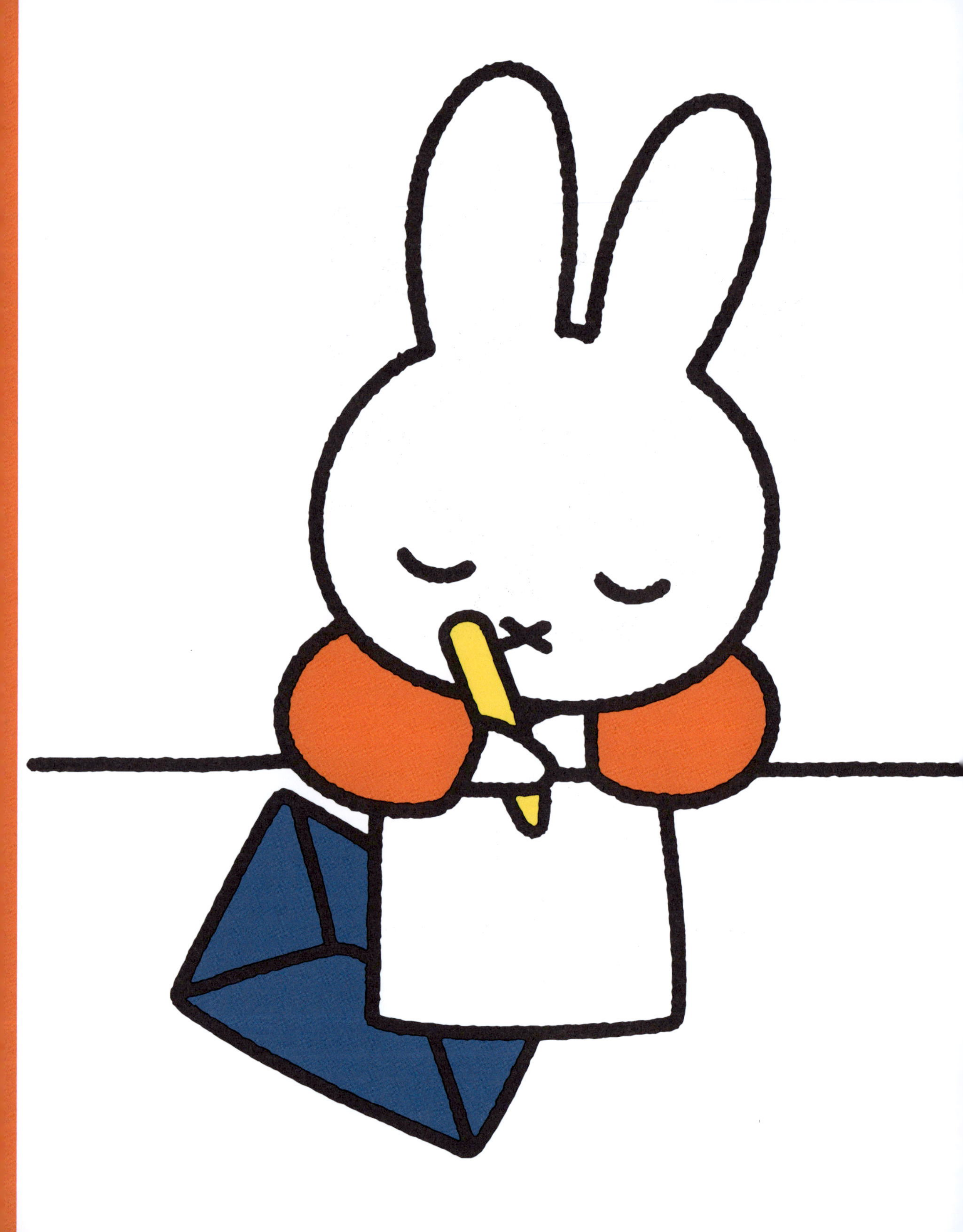

MIFFY

THE DESIGN PROCESS: FORM, LINE AND COLOUR

In 2003 Dick Bruna created *de brief van nijntje* (*miffy's letter*), one of his most adventurous and exciting books. Miffy goes camping with two friends and writes a letter home to tell them what she is doing. The pictures show her in different moods and she appears in a different setting each time. The book opens with a clinically white space where we encounter Miffy concentrating on writing her letter. Then we see her playing happily in Bruna-blue water. Shouting with joy in a group, she and her friends form a forest of rabbit ears surrounded by endless green. When she talks about the food, she is surrounded by a warm reddish-orange – a sensory manner of conveying the transition from outdoors to inside.

In 2011 Mercis bv and Bruna transferred the designs for *miffy's letter* to the Rijksmuseum on long-term loan. What makes these designs special is that they provide direct insight into Bruna's working methods. The sketches, collages, drawings and even films show all stages of the design process. These designs let us, as it were, look over Bruna's shoulder.

Different Stages of Design

Until he unexpectedly stopped drawing completely in 2012, Bruna cycled to his studio in Jeruzalemstraat in Utrecht at the crack of dawn every single day, including weekends. Everything there was arranged according to certain principles and in a fixed order. The well-nigh ritual acts lent the start of a working day an almost religious significance. The pencils were sharpened and laid in a neat row. The brushes were cleaned and placed within reach. His workbench was empty until he put his paper on it.

Bruna made the first sketch in pencil on almost transparent paper [FIG. 39]. He started with jerky lines, which let him try out several poses and looks. When he was happy – sometimes after hundreds of roughs – he took a thick sheet of watercolour paper. This sheet is placed underneath the transparent paper at the spot where Miffy had to be, usually in the middle. Then the pencil is traced over the lines again, so that the outlines are indented into the soft, rough-textured watercolour paper. The blueprint is complete.

And then something magical occurs. Like a craftsman, Bruna fills the incised groove with a brush dipped in black acrylic paint. The texture of the paper ensures that the slowly and carefully drawn line has a 'quiver' [FIG. 40]. This makes Miffy and her friends living beings: breathing and animated instead of static. Filling in the lines was time-consuming work, and if it did not come out precisely as Bruna had in mind, he started again. Perfectionism and discipline ensured the success of his prints.

Once he was satisfied, the final outlines were transferred on to a film photographically. This procedure became possible in 1963 and made a great difference to Bruna. He was able to lay the transparent sheet over a collage of different colours, for the clothes, background and other things [FIG. 41]. He cut out the colour fields from paper in standard Bruna colours. If a colour did not have the effect he wanted, he simply had to replace a piece of paper, without having to start the meticulously executed drawing all over again. He saw this approach, moving and replacing pieces of coloured paper, for the first time in Matisse's book *Jazz*.

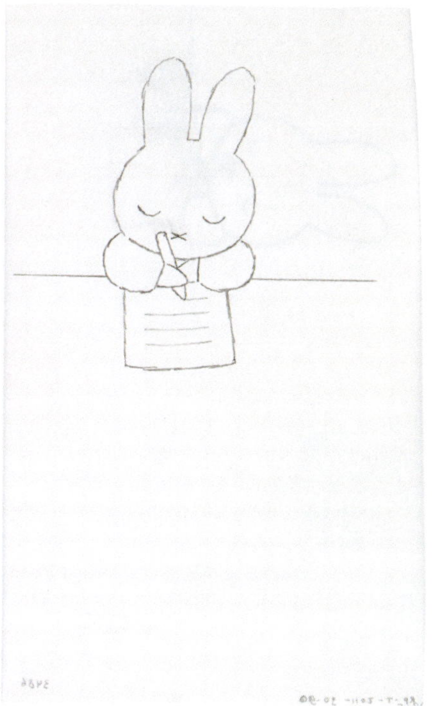

39 Dick Bruna
Miffy writing, sketch for
de brief van nijntje
(*miffy's letter*)
2003

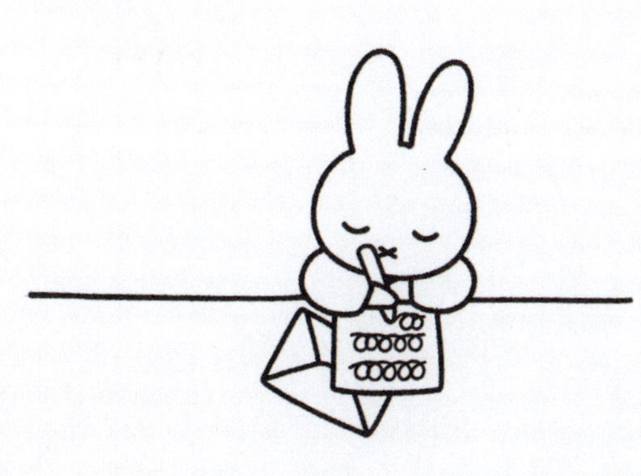

40 Dick Bruna
Miffy writing, study for
de brief van nijntje
(*miffy's letter*)
2003

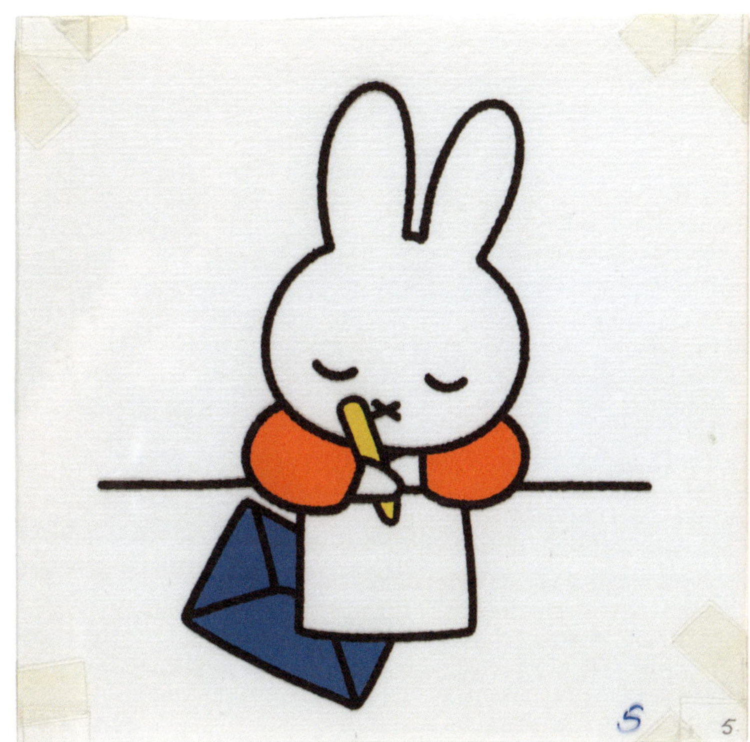

41 Dick Bruna
Miffy writing, cover design for
de brief van nijntje
(*miffy's letter*)
2003

Bruna's Theory of Colour

Because the compositions in the design stage could be seen in a few black lines as well as fields of colour, the impact of the green, red, yellow and blue could be seen at a glance. With outlines, uniform planes and simplicity, Bruna deliberately emphasized the flatness and two-dimensionality of a piece of paper. It is the colours that provide relative plasticity and provoke a sensory response. Bruna explained:

> 'Blue is a colour that recedes. It is a cool colour. Red and green come towards you. They are warm colours because there is yellow in them. When I draw children in a house, I give them a red or a yellow background. I want them to be warm in there.'

This corresponds with the theory of colour Johann Wolfgang von Goethe laid down in a scientific work published in 1810. He defined blue and violet as cold colours, as distinct from yellow and red, which are light and warm colours. The playwright and physician saw green as a neutral intermediate colour that was warm as well as cold, which seems self-evident given that it is a mixture of cold blue and warm yellow. The painter and colour theory expert Johannes Itten likewise described the contrast between yellow or red and blue as a warm-cold contrast. The blue background around these two rabbits splashing about comes across as cool [FIG. 42]: the feeling of temperature there is significantly lower than when they are eating [FIG. 43].

In this print neither of the rabbits is wearing a blue swimsuit, for reasons that have nothing to do with fashion. The colour would counteract the spatial effect; now it looks as if they are actually in the water instead of the water floating around them. The cheering rabbits in another print [FIG. 44] are wearing only primary colours for the same reason. They are surrounded by green above, below, left and right, while the area has to give the impression that the grass is actually under the rabbits' feet and that it extends to the invisible horizon. In our imagination the rabbits and the field are therefore in two spatial planes in different directions. This has to do not only with colour, but with the context and our expectations – we assume that it is grass: we do not see a green wall and floating rabbits. Yet there is not a single shadow, nor any linear perspective to give us specific indications of the surrounding scenery. Observation has to do not just with physiological processes, but above all with expectations, associations and experiences. This enables artists to abstract without losing touch with reality.

The decision to dress Miffy, the rabbit in front, in yellow is also a judicious one. The contrast of colour and warmth makes her appear closest to the viewer. And of course Miffy is the most striking because she is the only one not overlapped. In every case the use of colour was tailored to the situation and surroundings and can almost be described as archetypical. The sun is always yellow, the grass is always green and the sea is always blue. Occasionally the colour can have a symbolic significance. When Miffy is sad her usually red dress is blue.

Although the colours have been a constant in Bruna's oeuvre for more than half a century, they could change function and meaning according to how they were used. Consequently, they are never monotonous.

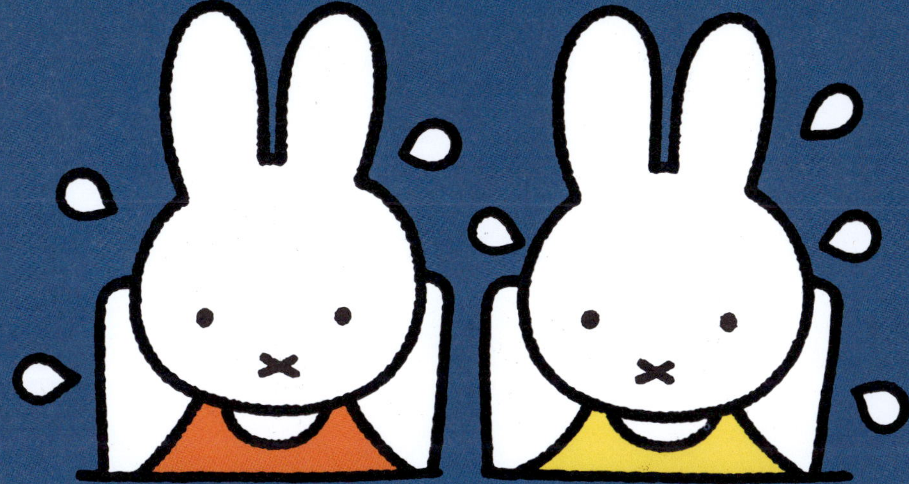

42 Dick Bruna
Miffy and friend in the water, design for *de brief van nijntje* (*miffy's letter*)
2003

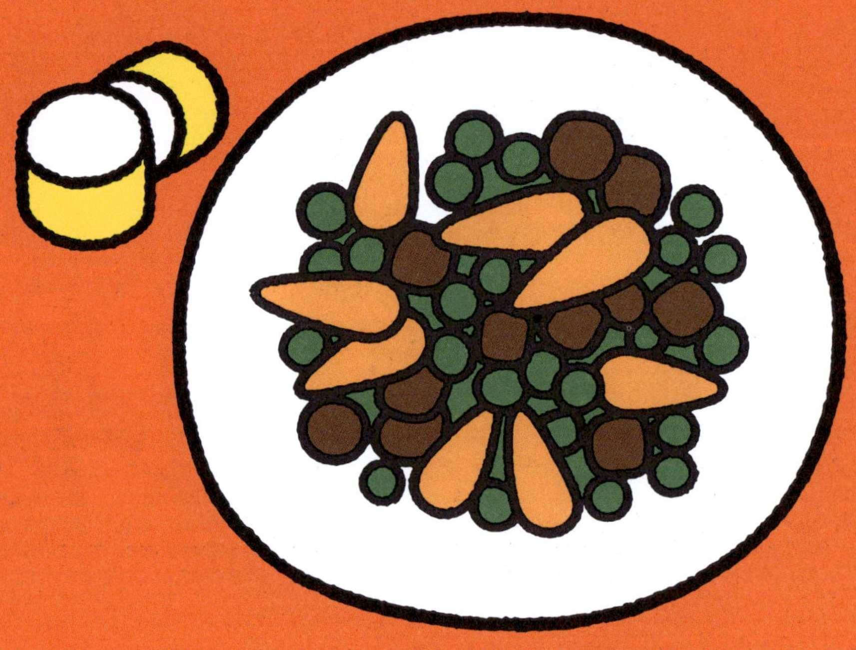

43 Dick Bruna
dinner plate, design for
de brief van nijntje
(*miffy's letter*)
2003

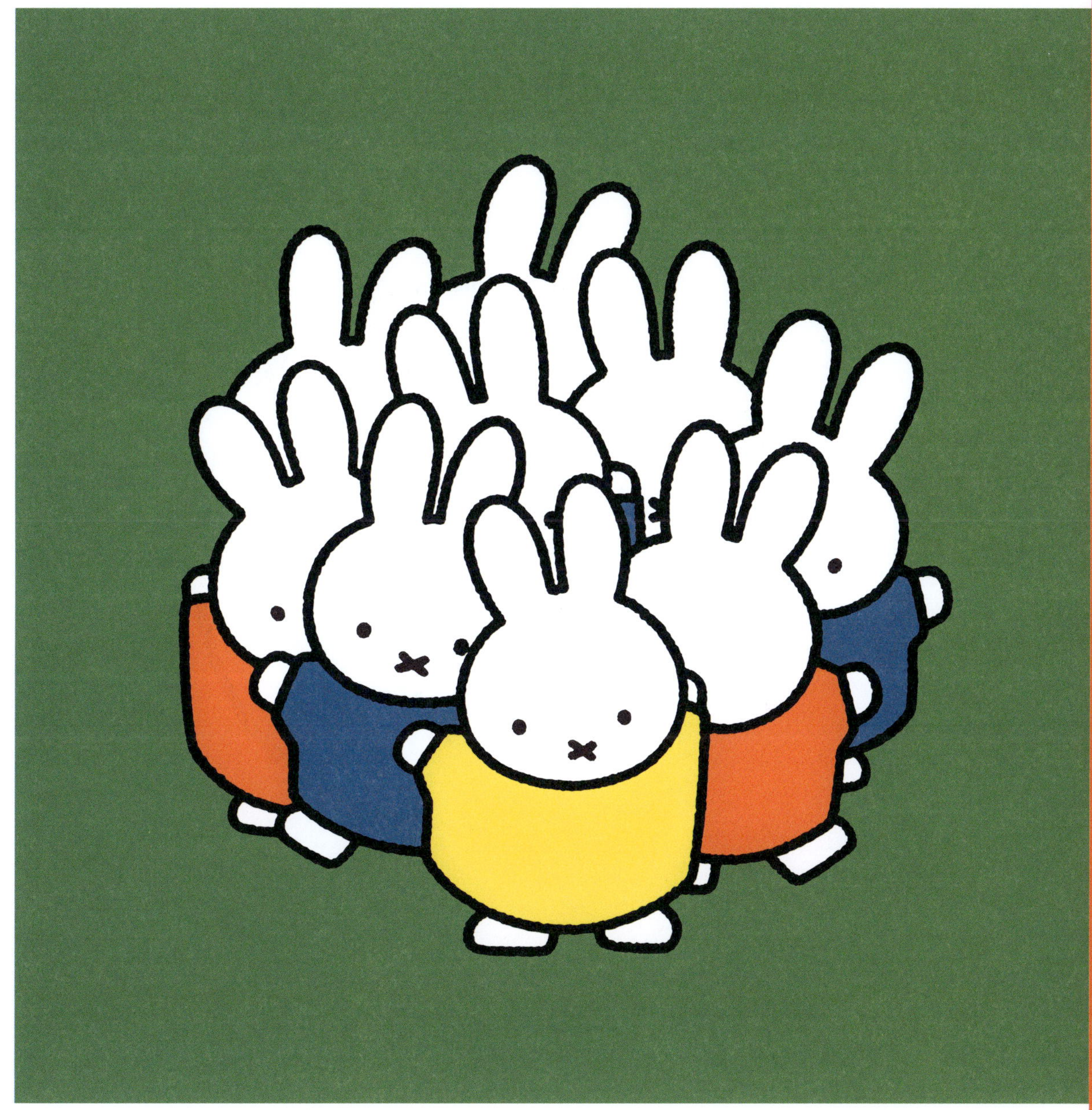

44 Dick Bruna
Miffy and friends dancing, design for *de brief van nijntje* (*miffy's letter*)
2003

THE MIFFY LINE

1955
Miffy (or actually, *nijntje*) sees the light. She does not yet look at the viewer. Her ears are wide apart and her eyes are placed low.

1963
The greatest metamorphosis. She now has oval ears, placed higher, and looks out at the viewer. She is relatively symmetrical and the design is spare. Her head is melon-shaped and wider at the bottom. Her appearance remains fairly stable until 1979.

1979
Starting with *nijntjes droom* (*miffy's dream*), her ears and face become slightly rounder.

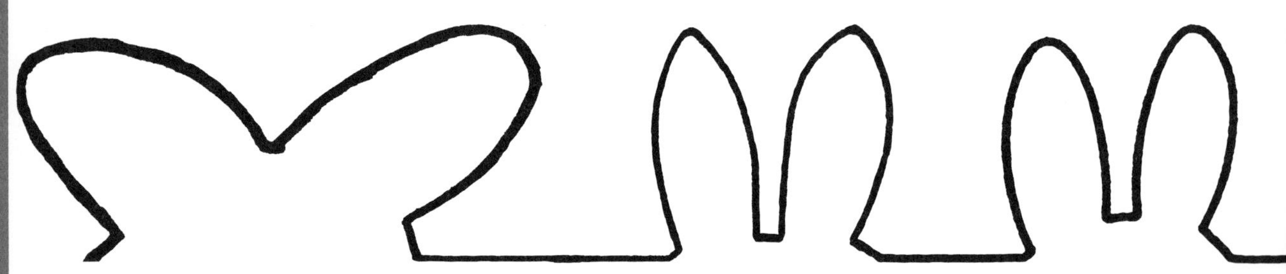

1955 1963 1979

1988
Everything about Miffy becomes a fraction rounder. Her mouth, the little cross, becomes slightly smaller.

1995
Her body becomes a little plumper and she seems to be slightly more compact. Her ears are considerably shorter.

2001
In *het spook nijntje* (*miffy the ghost*) the relationship between her head and body is modified. She starts to look more like a toddler. Her eyes are lower and the connection between her ears moves slightly higher.

2003
With the arrival of a sibling in *kleine pluis* (*the new baby*), Miffy becomes a big sister and a real youngster, with a high forehead, short round ears and a wider body. She has remained so into the most recent books.

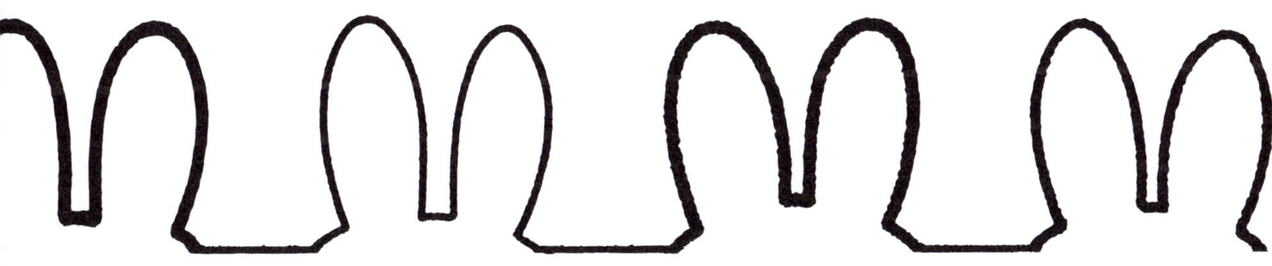

1988 1995 2001 2003

Miffy's Metamorphosis

Bruna drew Miffy (as *nijntje* got known outside the Netherlands since 1996) for the first time in 1955, during a summer holiday at Egmond aan Zee. The drawing was intended to amuse his one-year-old son. He may have been inspired by the real rabbits running around there, and those he remembered from his childhood. He could watch them for hours in his grandparents' garden. Although the first drawing of the little figure was intended for a child, in principle those that followed were not. Bruna always drew first and foremost for his own enjoyment. The first Miffy book was published in the very year she was created. From the moment the rectangular shape of the first book was transformed into a square in 1963, Miffy rose in popularity and this has only continued to increase. In total, Bruna made more than thirty books with her as the star: more than any of his other figures. Countless translations have brought international fame to the little girl rabbit.

Although she has hardly aged in more than fifty years, Miffy has undergone some significant changes in her appearance. These metamorphoses have given at least three generations all over the world a different perception of the same figure. Anyone born in the 1980s remembers Miffy with pointed ears set slightly apart. Children who were born after 2000 know the same rabbit with shorter, rounded ears that are upright. Nonetheless everyone, regardless of when she was drawn, recognizes the rabbit as Miffy. Like Father Christmas and Mickey Mouse, she is an archetypal character who has undergone small and larger changes over the years, but nevertheless remains instantly identifiable. Her mouth has always been a little cross and her eyes two dots. And for sixty years she has appeared in an unchanging combination of colours.

What strikes one immediately is that Bruna did not produce a cuddly bunny for the first version of Miffy, but sought the kind of iconic abstraction seen in the work of Matisse and Léger. Yet this first version is the most three-dimensional rendition in which she was ever to appear [FIG. 46]. The snout protrudes slightly, as is the case in real animals. Her eyes look away from the viewer. The flat Miffy we know did not appear for another eight years.

In 1963, the year of the greatest changes, Miffy looks straight at the viewer [FIG. 45]. She has become streamlined and slightly more symmetrical. Her ears stand proudly upright. This make-over was the decisive factor in her breakthrough. Although adults in the 1960s did not think much of the simple figure – at that time other children's books were drawn in quite considerable detail – children were instantly attracted by the Modernist visual idiom of simplicity and clarity.

The larger and slimmer her body, the longer ago she was drawn. If her head is wide and the eyes are high up, we are looking at an older example from the 1960s or '70s. Her ears were most pointed in the first half of the 1960s. In the decades that followed, she became shorter and rounder. Her eyes drop down a little more and move wider apart. In the 1990s there was a halt in these changes.

The metamorphosis of 1988 – when her ears clearly became shorter and rounder – was the second radical change and the last with great impact. The smaller changes from 2003 when she became much plumper and more compact completed this development. The changes were unusual, because in a number of respects Miffy reverted to her original character. For example, she was again given the high forehead with which she came into the world in 1955. From a slim, pointy rabbit, she had become 'nicely rounded'.

Bruna cannot put his finger on what provoked this need for small and larger transformations. They just happened, and he followed what occurred to him. He is, though, able to sum up the general trend in the changes: 'I think my rabbit definitely became more human over the years'.[18]

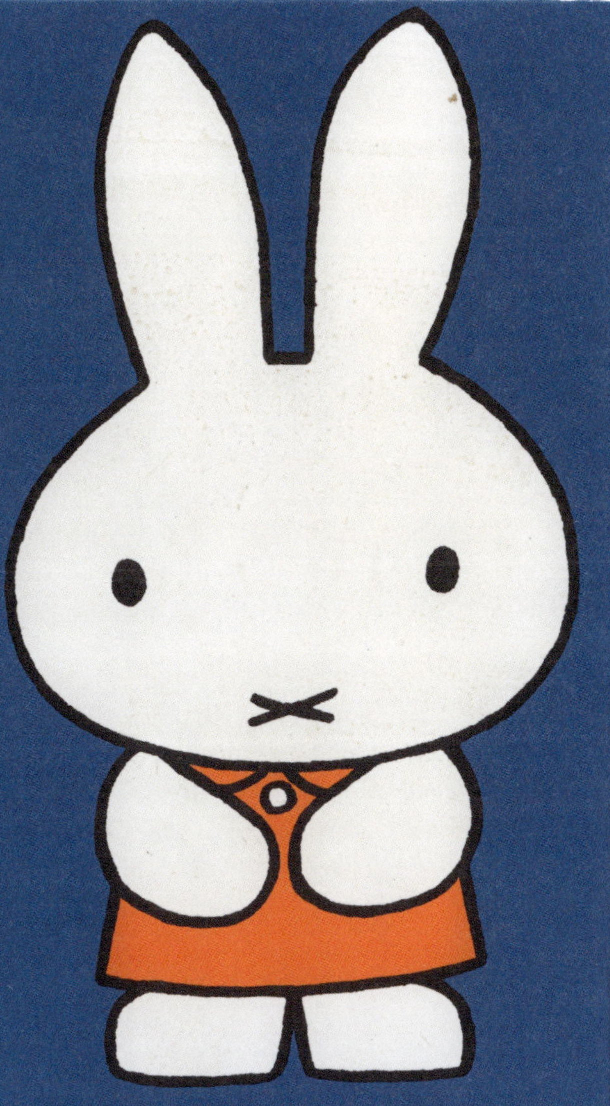

45 Dick Bruna
cover of *nijntje* (*miffy*)
book 16
1963

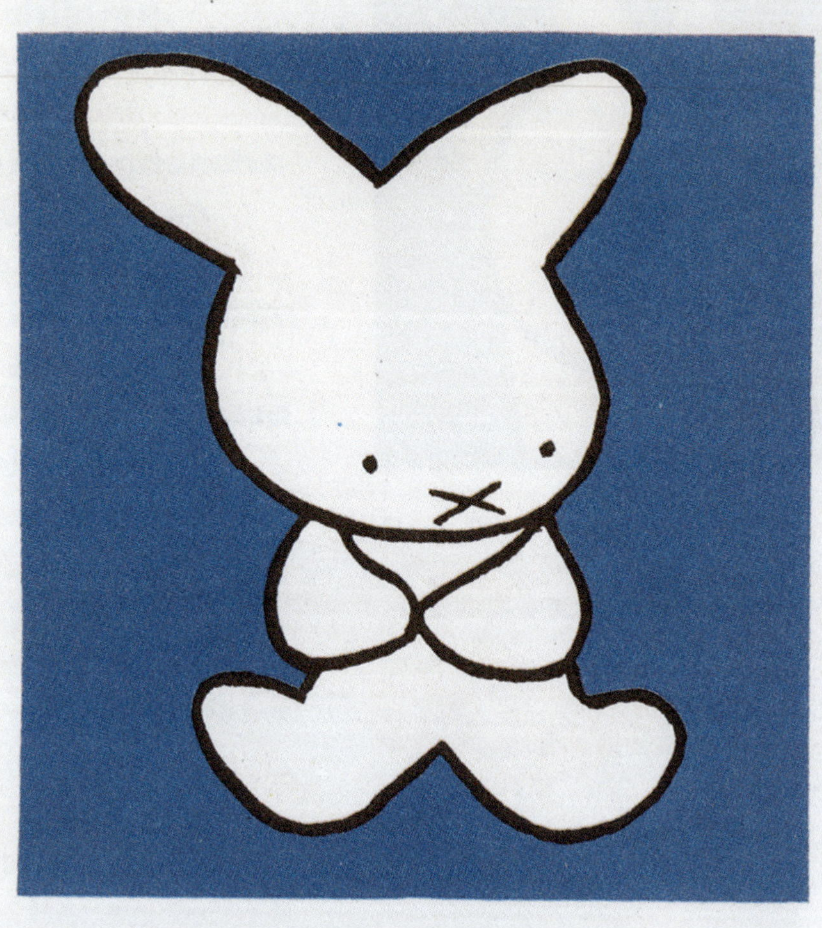

46 Dick Bruna
pages from the first
Miffy publication
book 1
1955

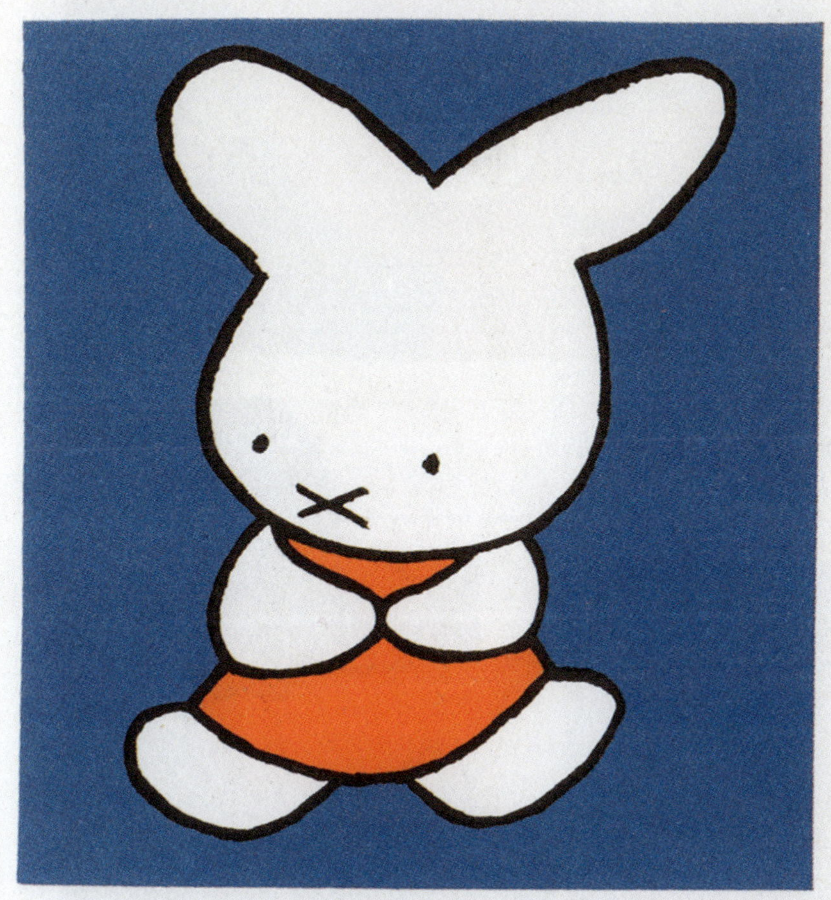

zij trokken haar een jurkje aan
en noemden haar toen Nijntje

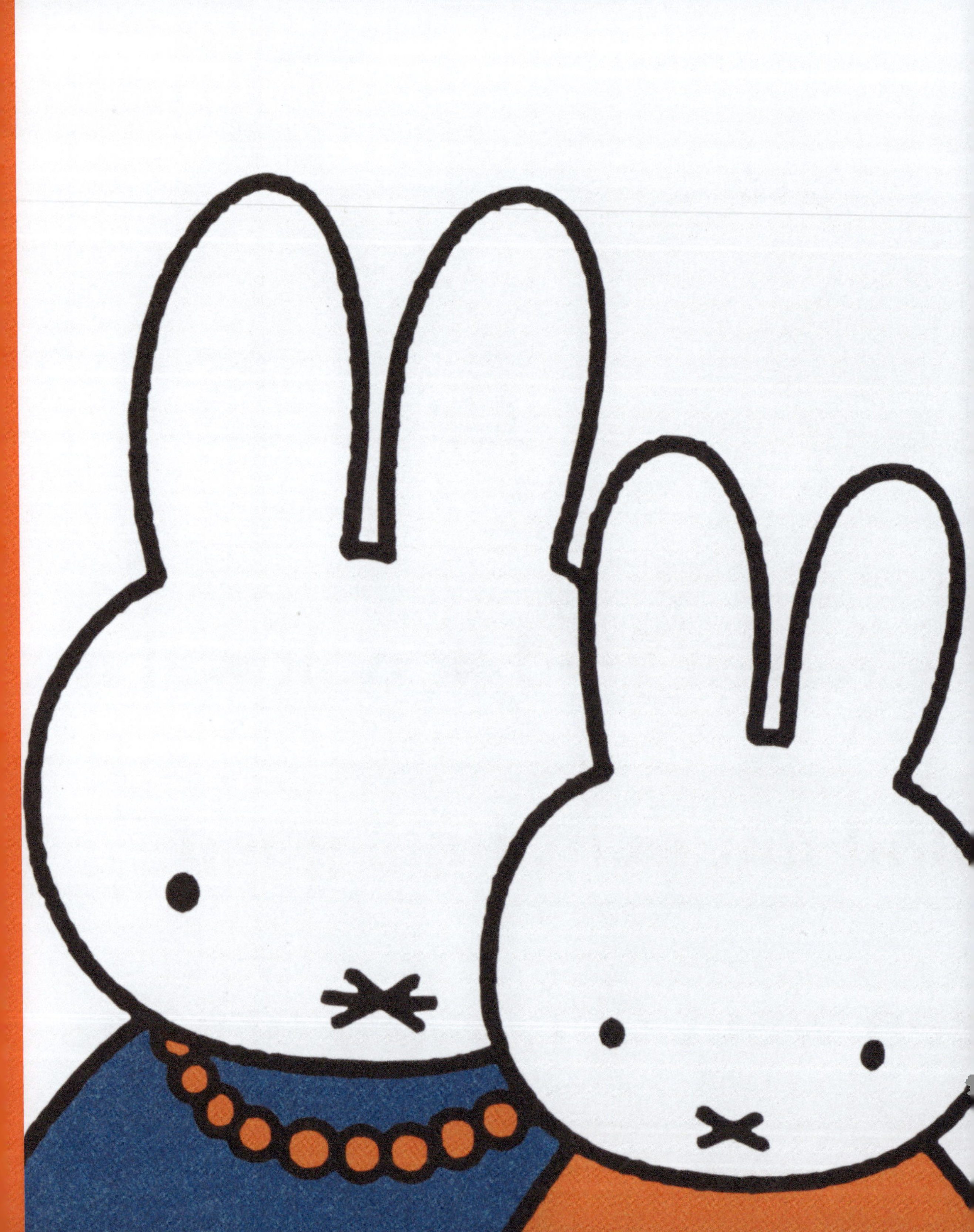

60 YEARS OF MIFFY: HUMAN AND UNIVERSAL

At first, Miffy's face may appear immobile and void of intense emotions. She has no eyebrows with which to express herself, no real corners to her mouth or wrinkles and laugh lines. She has only a little cross that acts as her nose and mouth, two dots as eyes and two proud ears that stand motionless on her head. Nevertheless Bruna always adjusts Miffy's face with the few elements he had at his disposal. Painstakingly, with meticulous care, often extremely subtly, he slaves away for hours with a brush and black paint to model the 'quivering line' he so cherishes into an animated, thinking and feeling being. During the last sixty years of her existence, the little rabbit has been surprised, sad, cross, ashamed and happy. She has celebrated, stolen, mourned and atoned for her sins.

But how is it possible for us to make out the face of a living being in two dots and two tiny crossed lines? In *Art and Illusion: A Study in the Psychology of Pictorial Representation*, art historian Ernst Gombrich maintained that two simple points are enough to suggest eyes because in evolutionary terms it was a matter of life and death to be able to identify a predator watching us. This is why even without irises, whites of the eyes or eyelids, the two black points on Miffy's face give us the feeling she is looking at us.

What is more, we can recognize not just animation, but several emotions in the very abstract little figure. In 1872 the renowned evolutionary biologist Charles Darwin published his pioneering work *The Expression of the Emotions in Man and Animals.* Based on detailed illustrations of faces of humans and animals, Darwin linked emotion to universal facial expressions. For example, he described slightly compressed lips – like Miffy's cross when she looks at art [FIG. 47] – as a universal expression of concentration. Although cultural historians have meanwhile demonstrated that the interpretation of emotions can differ, both between different cultures and down through the ages, there are also great similarities that are universal and timeless. And Bruna appears to be able to translate them instinctively.

An experiment carried out among the curators of the Rijksmuseum shows how a minimal shift in the position of the dots and cross on the little rabbit's face can affect it. A number of Rijksmuseum curators – by definition visually attuned – were asked to draw Miffy's mouth and eyes from memory [FIG. 48]. It was much more difficult than they had expected. The result demonstrated that the tiniest of shifts in mouth and eyes were able to create totally different expressions. Most of the little rabbits looked rather surprised, dissatisfied or not all there.

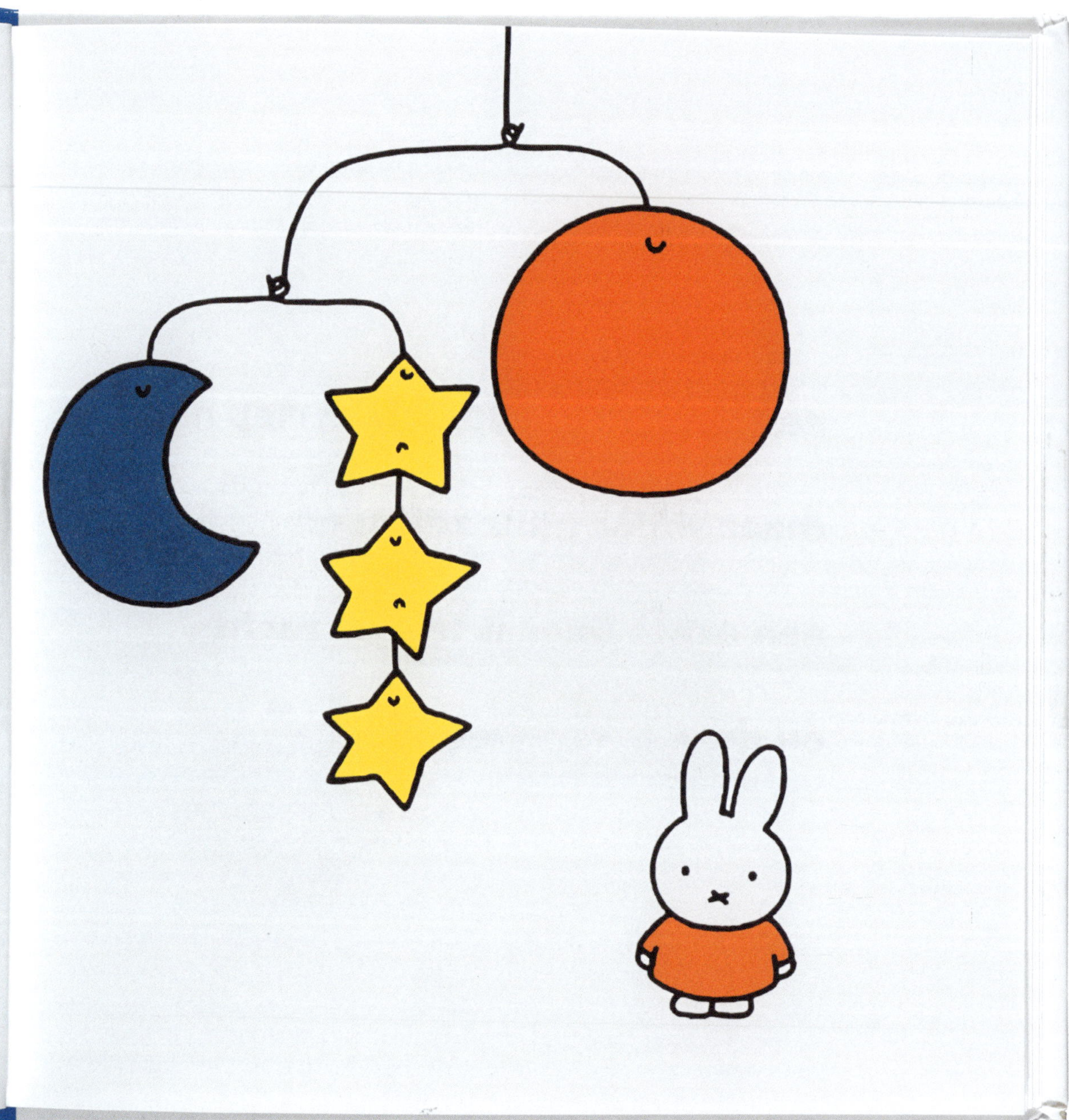

47 Dick Bruna
Miffy and Calder,
in *nijntje in het museum*
(*miffy at the gallery*)
1997

48 Rijksmuseum curators drew the eyes and cross in the outline of Miffy's face

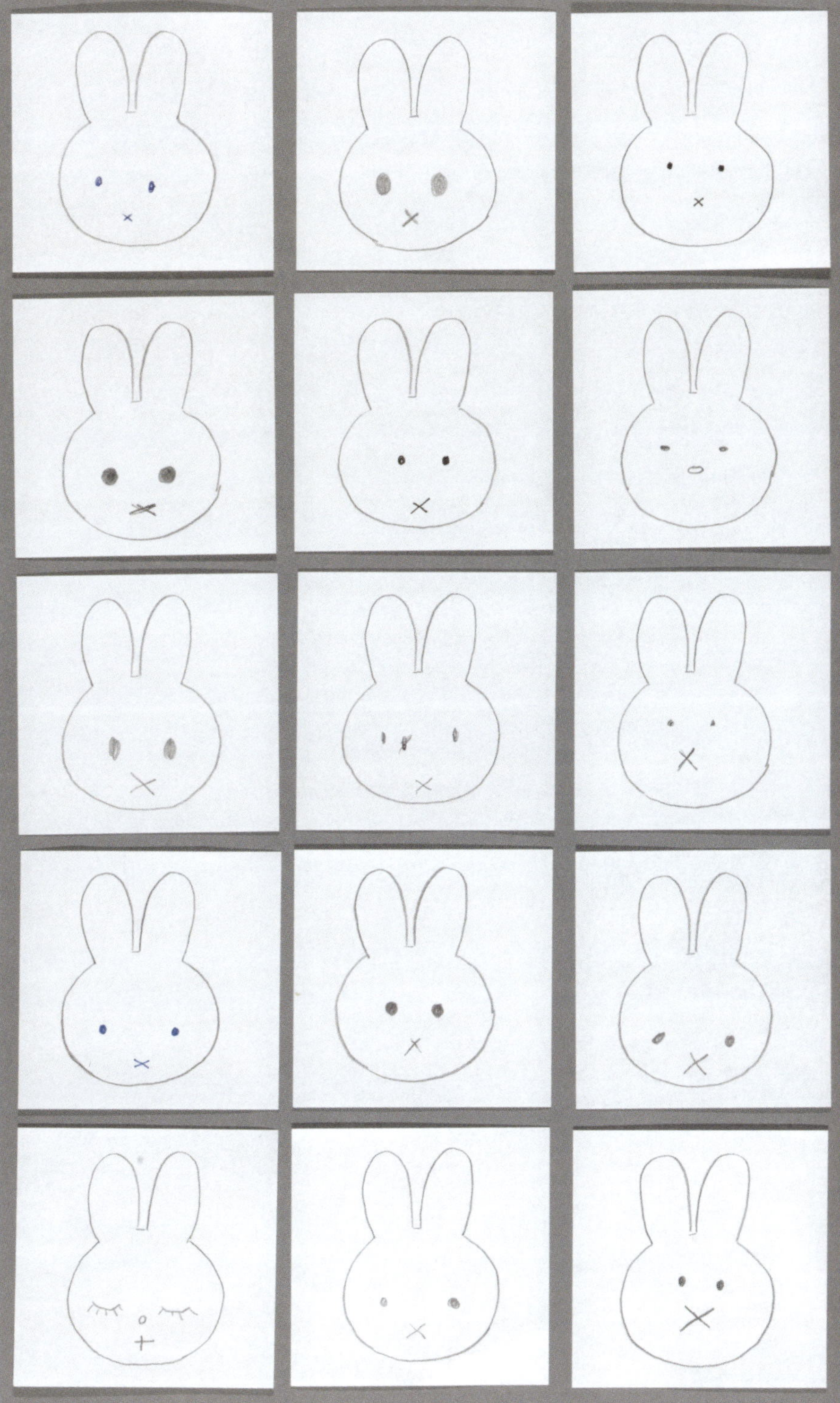

Amazement and Satisfaction

In *nijntje in het museum* (*miffy at the gallery*) Miffy visits a museum with her parents. At the beginning her father wonders if she is really big enough to go to a serious place like a museum. Luckily she manages to convince him: 'too small, said miffy, no I'm not/ I'm really big and tall!' The family sets off at once. In the accompanying caption there is a clue to her emotional state, 'so miffy was allowed to go/ and off the bunnies went/ what fun to see a gallery/ miff wondered what it meant'. Bruna drew her expectant curiosity by making her eyes bigger – longer and wider [FIG. 50A]. A very human and animal reaction: fear, suspense and excitement make the pupils larger so perception sharpens. After she has admired the modern masters, it is time to go home. On the way back, the black dots become noticeably smaller [FIG. 50B]. The suspense and excitement are replaced by satisfaction. Although it is so subtle as to be barely apparent, the intervention is effective.

Miffy's flat face and eyes without irises could even indicate a direction of gaze when they were depicted frontally. In the illustration in which she and her mother are looking at two horizontal compositions (references to a Bruna print from the 1990s, *boris op de berg* (*boris on the mountain*), Miffy's face appears to tilt forward [FIG. 49]. The circle that forms her head is a little wider at the top, as if it was placed in perspective, so the forehead seems to be a little closer to the observer. To emphasize the direction of view, the eyes are slightly lower than in the first frontal portrait of Miffy on the way to the gallery. The cross is drawn a little more finely and flatter than in the first illustration.

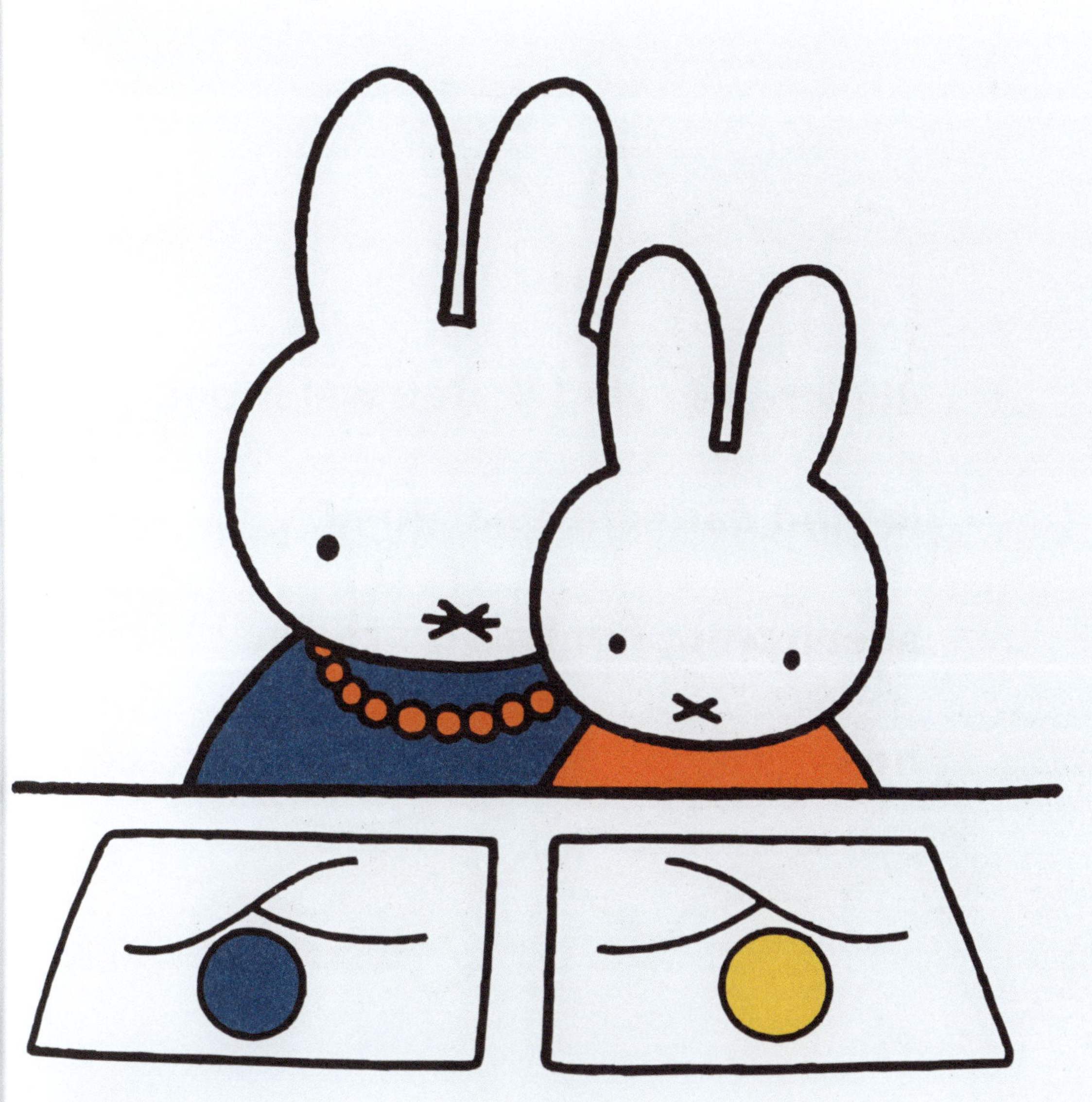

49 Dick Bruna
Miffy and her mother,
in *nijntje in het museum*
(*miffy at the gallery*)
1997

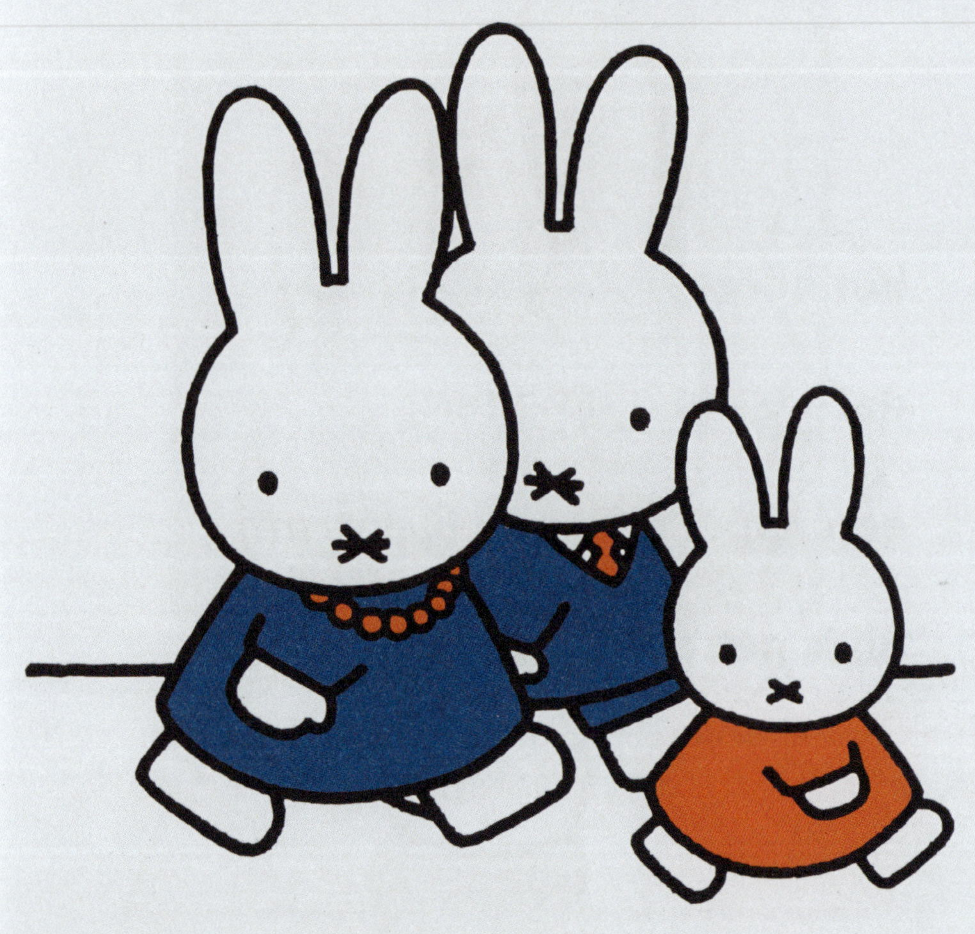

50A, B
Dick Bruna
off to the museum and
walking back home,
in *nijntje in het museum*
(*miffy at the gallery*)
1997

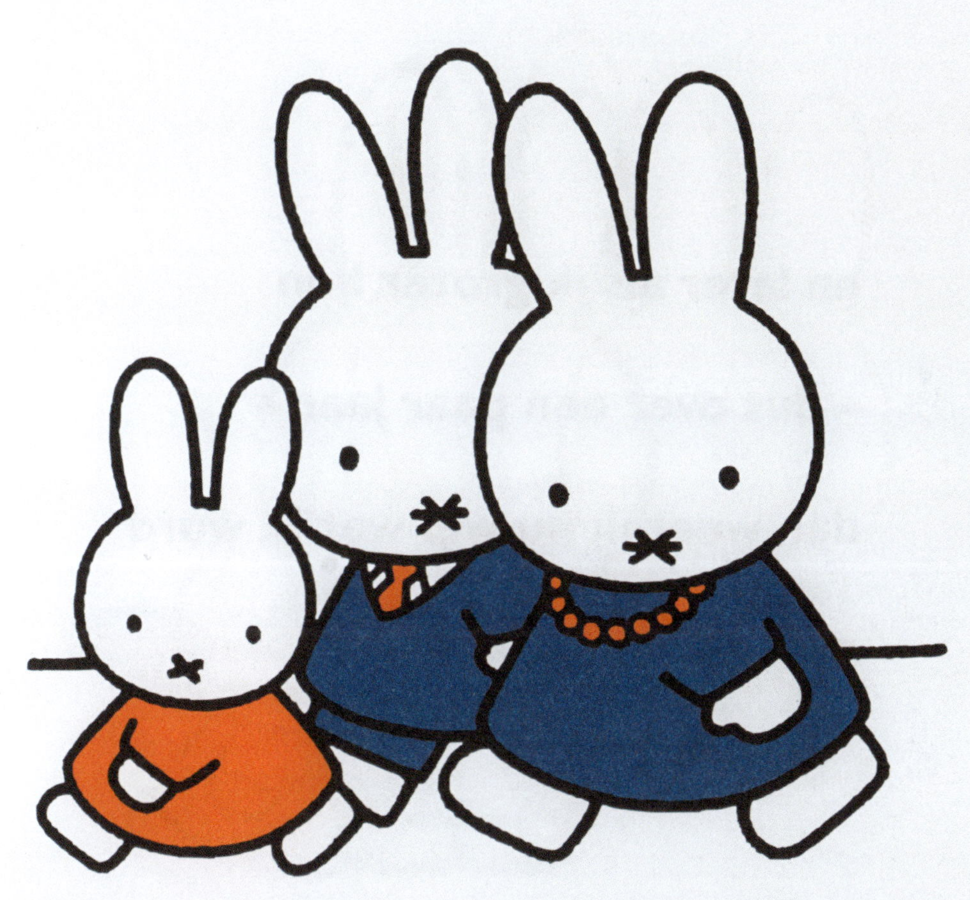

Shame and Regret

In *nijntje is stout* (*miffy is naughty*), the generally well-behaved Miffy steals some toffees from a shop. Immediately before she does it, we see her looking round the cake shop. The fact that she is concentrating on something is shown from the relatively short distance between her eyes ('while mother bought the biscuits/ miffy just looked around/ till in a corner of the shop/ a bowl of sweets she found') [FIG. 51A]. The corners of her mouth are wide apart and turned up a little. She is excited about the colourfully wrapped sweets. In the next illustration the deed has just been done: the stolen sweets are sticking out of her pocket [FIG. 51B]. Now the nose-mouth cross is shorter and flatter. Turned-in corners of the mouth indicate tension and frustration: the flattened lips tell us that Miffy is on her guard. She is standing stock still so as not to give herself away by making a noise. Her eyes are smaller and rounder and further apart than in the previous picture. Darwin believed that someone who feels guilty narrows his or her eyes slightly. The image overflows with terror and a sense of guilt. The sideways position of her body indicates that she is looking over her shoulder: a sign of alertness – or a guilty conscience.

The fact that Miffy is sorry for what she did and even afraid can be seen in the illustration in which she is in bed at night and peeping over the blankets [FIG. 52]. The cutting-off of the eyes – she hardly dares look – is telling. The usually white, innocent rabbit takes on the colour of her surroundings. She is swallowed up by the darkness. This emphasizes the oppressive feeling that afflicts Miffy at this moment, 'but once in bed you'll understand/ she lay there all night long/ and all she thought was I'm a thief/ that's stupid and it's wrong.'

After she confesses to her mother, who had been alerted by her suspicious behaviour, Miffy returns the sweets, 'so at the baker's miffy put/ the sweeties back and then/ she said now I will never do/ a thing like that again'.

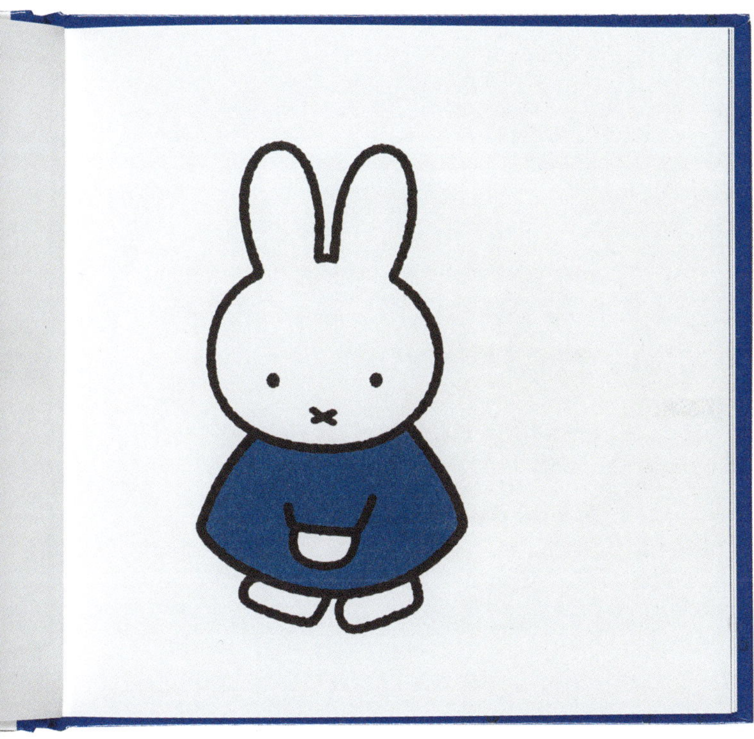

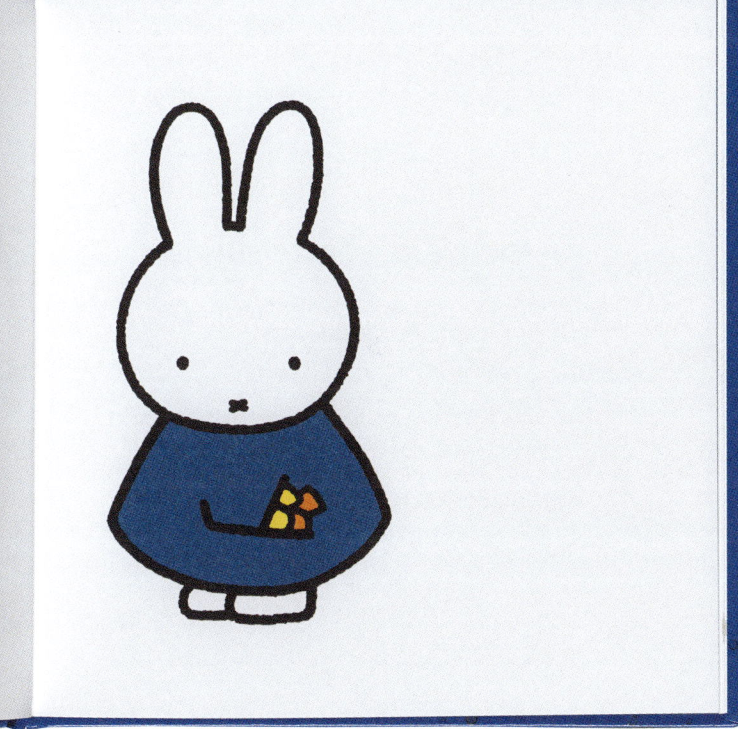

51A, B
Dick Bruna
Miffy on the look-out and
Miffy stealing, in *nijntje is stout*
(*miffy is naughty*)
2007

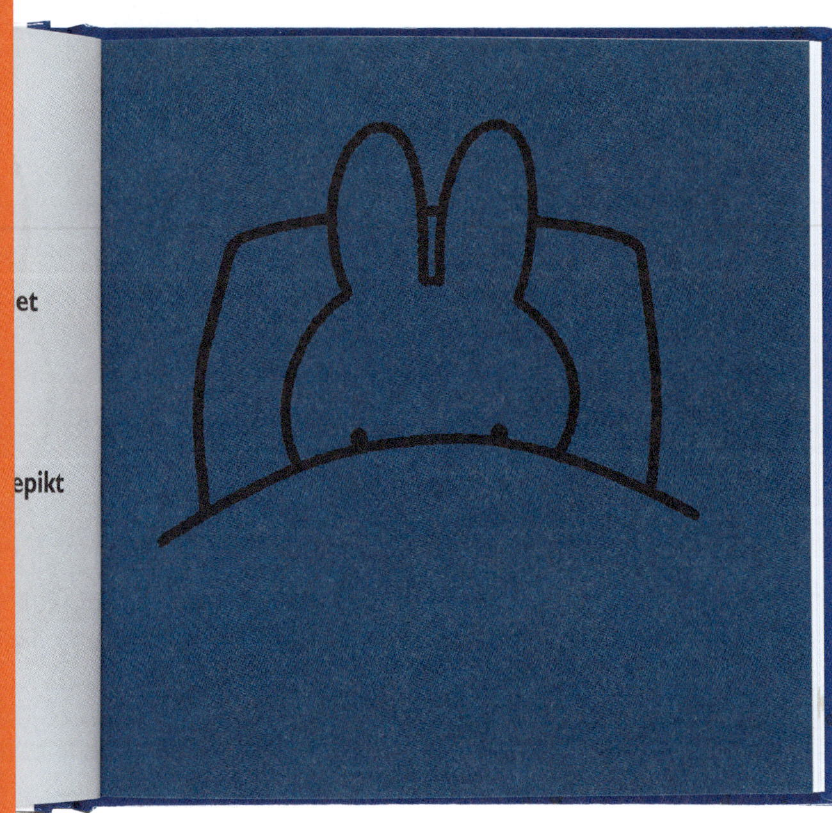

52 Dick Bruna
Miffy in bed, in *nijntje is stout*
(*miffy is naughty*)
2007

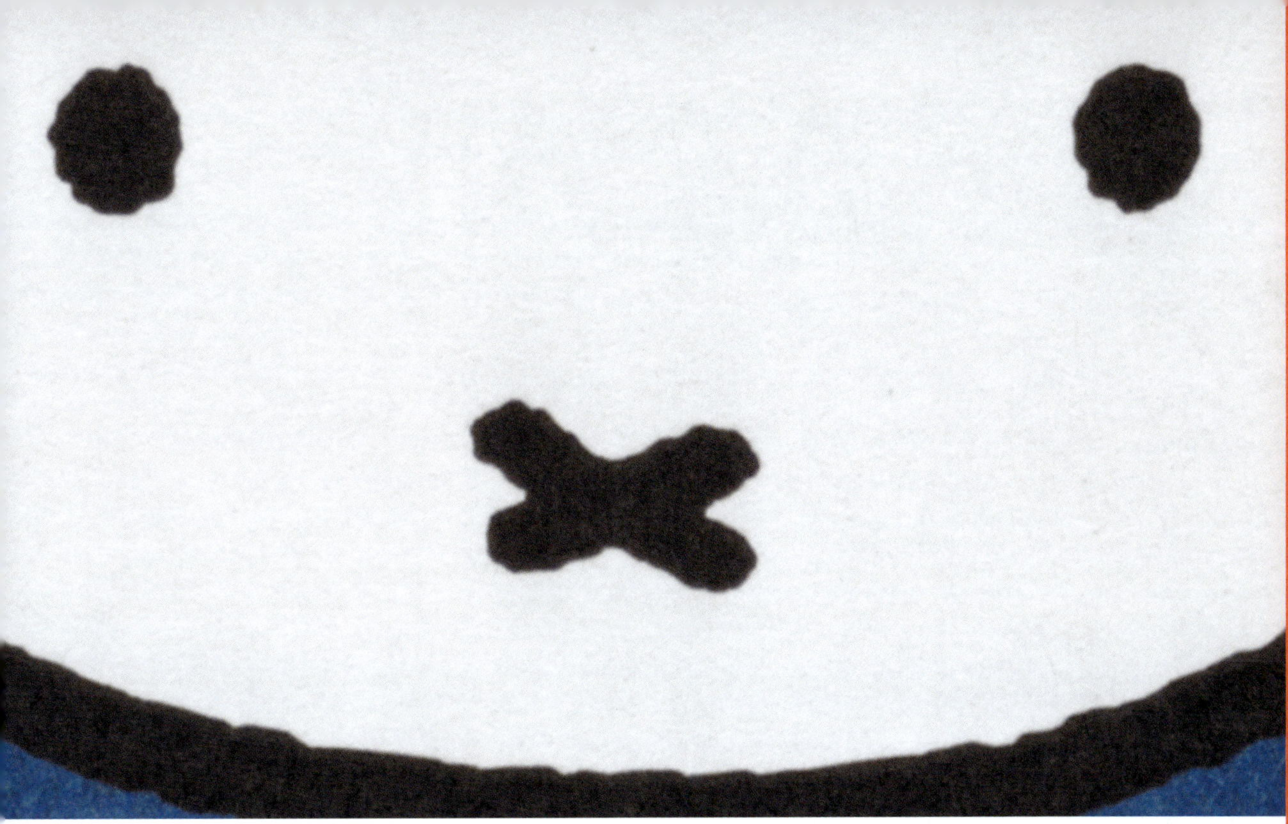

details of figs. 51A, B

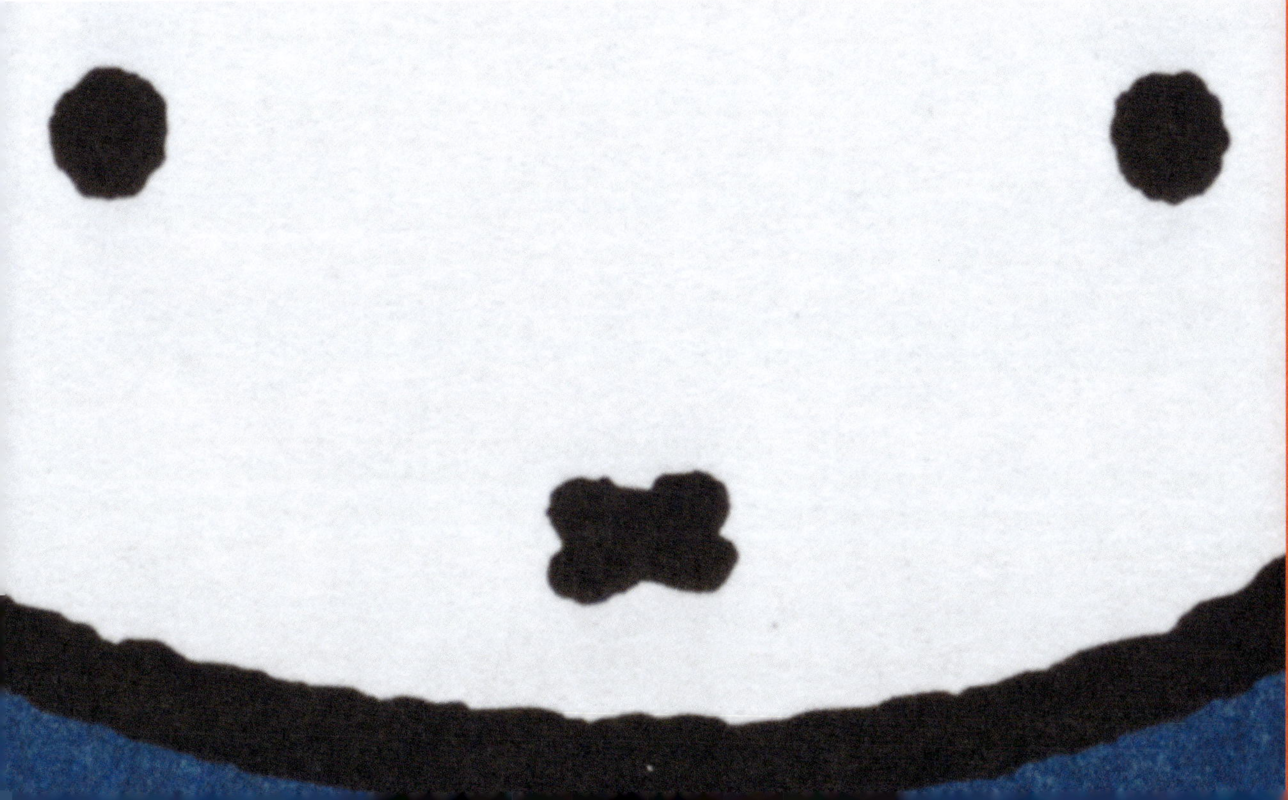

Sorrow

why was miffy so unhappy?
on her cheek a tear was bright
do you know why she was crying?
miffy's grandma died last night

As well as excitement, guilt and fear, the little rabbit experiences different forms of sadness. Sometimes her tears are caused by disappointment, as in *nijntje huilt* (*miffy is crying*), in which she loses her teddy-bear [FIG. 53]. But sometimes they are generated by the all-consuming grief for the loss of a fellow creature. In *lieve oma pluis* (*dear grandma bunny*), her grandmother dies. The little rabbit's eyes are drawn a little more raggedly, as if they are cloudy [FIG. 54]. Her mouth consists of thick lines and although they are longer than when she feels guilty, they are horizontally placed. They even droop a little. Darwin identified drooping corners of the mouth as a sign of sorrow and fear. In her various capacities, Miffy – in all her humanity – holds a mirror to her readers.

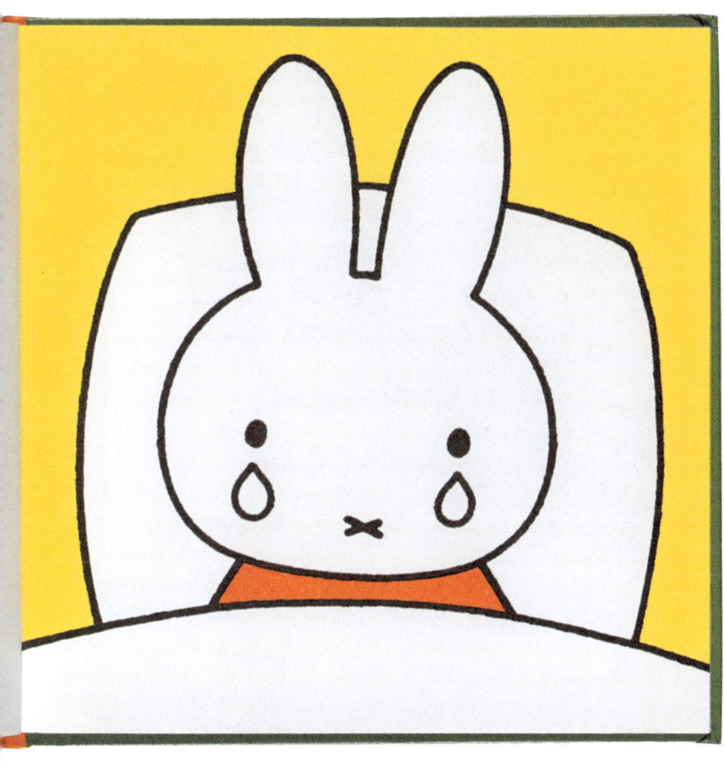

53 Dick Bruna
Miffy crying over the loss of her teddybear, in *nijntje huilt* (*miffy is crying*)
1991

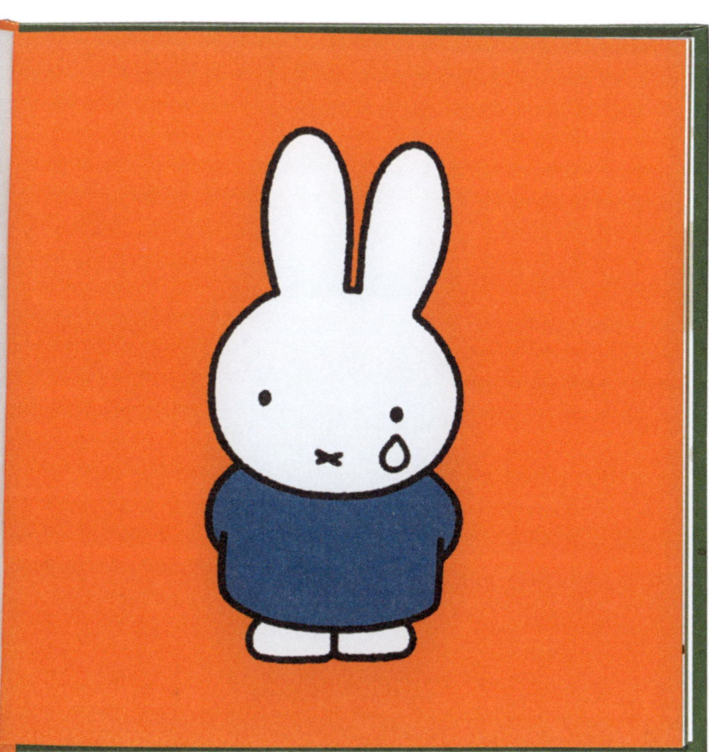

54 Dick Bruna
Miffy crying over her grandmother's death, in *lieve oma pluis* (*dear grandma bunny*)
1996

DICK BRUNA ARTIST

The influence of the art of the first half of the twentieth century resonates in Dick Bruna's book covers, posters, drawings and books of prints. In his famous Miffy, above all, we see how he brings many historical influences together to create a unique entity that cites none of them verbatim. Whereas Mondrian, for example, rarely used round shapes, Matisse did not compose according to a geometric principle. Sandberg's influence is evident in the lower case sans-serif letters used in Bruna's square print books, whereas there are ornamental letters on the covers. He based the iconic character of his figures on work by such artists as Werkman, but the atmosphere remained his own.

Although it was the design idiom that inspired Bruna above all, he also shared a certain idealism with his predecessors and contemporaries. The historic avant-garde broke away from the styles of the past, abandoning perspective, dissolving the difference between foreground and background and increasing abstraction and expression. The avant-garde saw abstraction as a means of achieving an ideal society. The creation of a 'visual Esperanto' would create accessibility that would go beyond culture and could change the world.

We see Bruna's idealistic leanings in his books of prints. They bring to life a world where harmony, kindness and warmth predominate. Bruna, like Matisse, was primarily interested in evoking a sense of cheerful light-heartedness, not the drama and passion we associate with 'high art'. And yet there is also room for universal emotions like sadness, shame and even grief. The simplicity of the expression allows each individual to project his or her own feelings.

The worldwide appreciation of Miffy says something about mankind's amazing capacity to translate clear lines, planes and proportions into feelings we all recognize. However, the ease with which we can do this says much more about the talent of an artist who knows how to reduce the complex to the essential. It is perhaps for this very reason that people of many nationalities, and the youngest, too, understand his pictorial language.

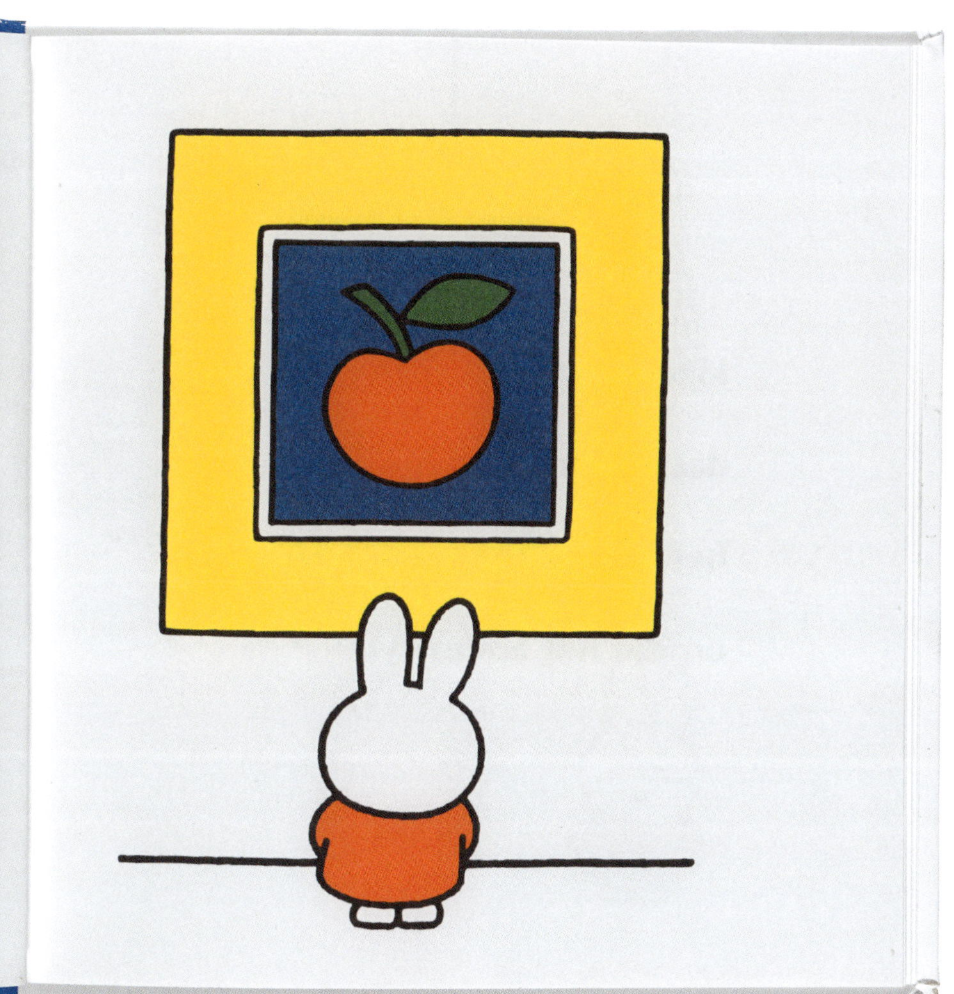

55 Dick Bruna
Miffy and apple,
in *nijntje in het museum*
(*miffy at the gallery*)
1997

Is Miffy looking at an original work by the artist Dick Bruna?

NOTES

1 J. Linders and K. Sierman 2011, p. 111

2 Dick Bruna, interview in *Elsevier*, 10 November 2007

3 Dick Bruna, interview in *NRC Handelsblad*, 30 October 1992

4 Dick Bruna, in the documentary *Icon & Inspiration – Dick Bruna Worldwide*, 2005. Production: Human Factor Television Products, commissioned by Mercis bv

5 Ibid.

6 Dick Bruna, interview in *Het Parool*, 4 July 1992

7 Dick Bruna, see note 4

8 B. Jansen, *Dick Bruna – Boekomslagen*, exh. cat. Utrecht (Centraal Museum) 2000

9 Dick Bruna, interview in *Het Parool*, 4 July 1992

10 C. Rutten 2011, p. 61

11 Ibid., p. 62

12 Dick Bruna, interview in *de Volkskrant*, 7 January 2011

13 H. Steenbruggen 1996

14 Dick Bruna, see note 4

15 E. Reitsma and K. Nieuwenhuijzen, *Het paradijs in pictogram: Het werk van Dick Bruna*, Amsterdam 1989, p. 55

16 D. van Vrie, *Kwadraat-bladen 1955–74*, Amsterdam 2005

17 With thanks to Rijksmuseum curator Ludo van Halem for this insight

18 Dick Bruna, see note 4

LITERATURE

K. Buchberg et al. (eds.) *Henri Matisse: The Cut-Outs*, exh. cat. New York (MoMA) 2014

C. Darwin, *The Expression of the Emotions in Man and Animals,* London 1872

E. Gombrich, *Art and Illusion: A Study in the Psychology of Pictorial Representation,* London 1977

E. Hoek, *Theo van Doesburg*, exh. cat. Otterlo (Kröller-Müller Museum)/Utrecht (Centraal Museum) 2000

B. Jansen, *Dick Bruna – Boekomslagen*, exh. cat. Utrecht (Centraal Museum) 2000

T. van Kooten, *Bart van der Leck*, exh. cat. Otterlo (Kröller-Müller Museum) 1994

J. Linders and K. Sierman, *Dick Bruna*, Zwolle 2006

K. Löb, 'Dick (Bruna) (Dutch designer)', *Novum*, March 1973, pp. 42–7

K. Nieuwenhuizen and E. Reitsma, *Het paradijs in pictogram: Het werk van Dick Bruna*, Amsterdam 1989

C. Rutten, *Gesprekken met Dick Bruna*, Amsterdam 2011

H. Steenbruggen, *The Smell of Success*, exh. cat. Groningen (Groninger Museum) 1996

C. Vermaas and S. Zijlstra (eds.), *Dick Bruna*, Eindhoven 2011

K. Yanagimoto, *Zwarte Beertjes: De boekomslagen van Dick Bruna / Black Bear: Book Cover Designs by Dick Bruna / Black Bear: Dick Bruna no soutei no shigoto*, Tokyo 2004

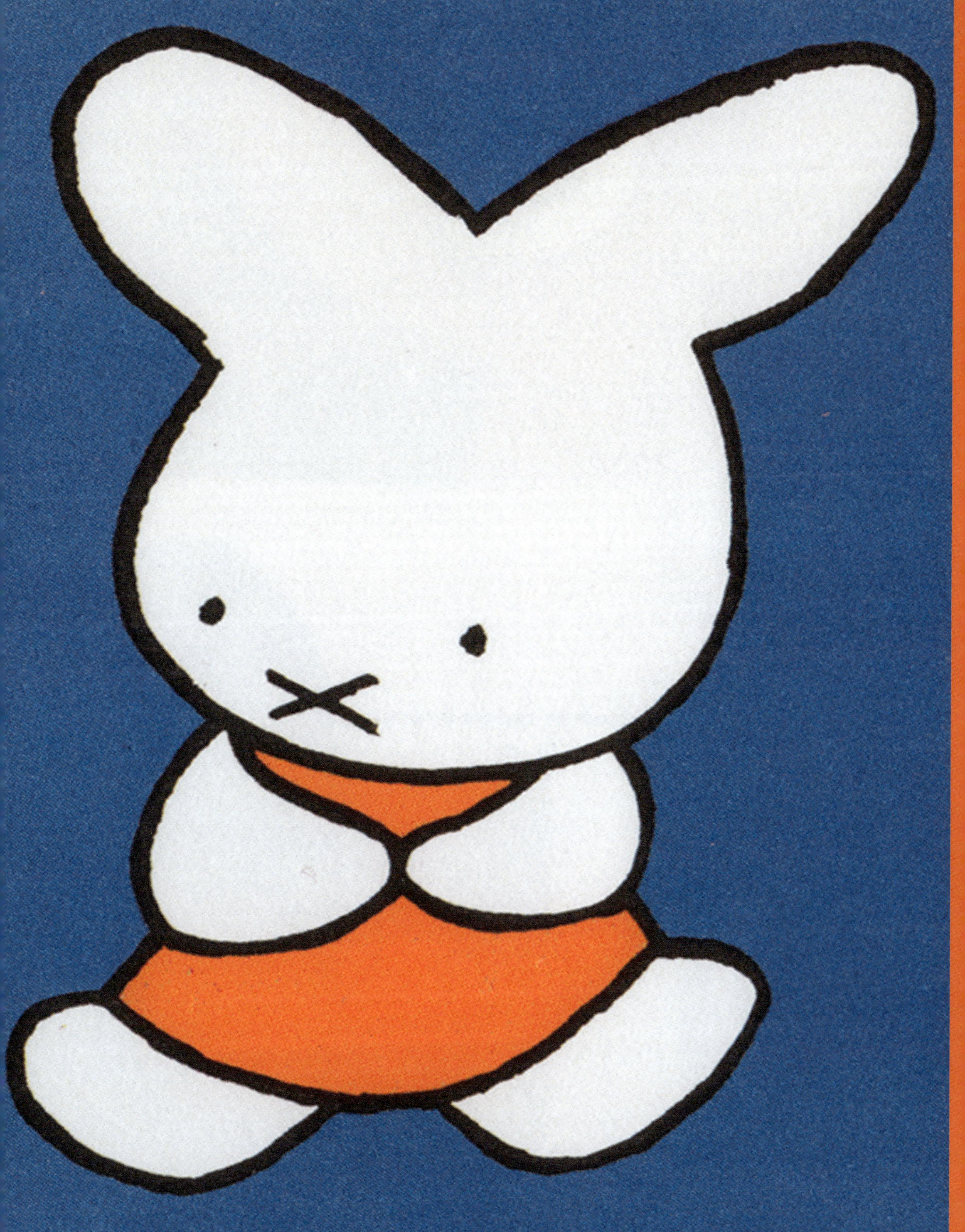

LIST OF ILLUSTRATIONS

1 Dick Bruna during his visit to the Rijksmuseum restoration workshop in 2011

2A, B
Dick Bruna
cover design for
Georges Simenon,
Maigret en de gangsters
(*Maigret and the Gangsters*)
1970
Collage and film, 183 x 118 mm
Utrecht (A.W. Bruna & Zn.)
Amsterdam, Rijksmuseum
Inv. no. RP-P-2011-125-35;
on loan from D. Bruna, Utrecht, and Mercis bv

Dick Bruna
cover for Georges Simenon,
De woede van Maigret
(*Maigret Loses His Temper*)
1964
Letterpress, 175 x 115 mm
Utrecht (A.W. Bruna & Zn.)
Amsterdam, Rijksmuseum
Inv. no. RP-P-2011-125-12;
on loan from D. Bruna, Utrecht, and Mercis bv

3A, B
Dick Bruna
cover design for Havank,
Circus Mikkenie
1965
Collage, 180 x 118 mm
Utrecht (A.W. Bruna & Zn.)
Amsterdam, Rijksmuseum
Inv. no. RP-T-2011-90-96;
on loan from D. Bruna, Utrecht, and Mercis bv

Dick Bruna
cover design for Havank,
De Schaduw is terug
(*The Shadow Returns*)
1966
Letterpress, 175 x 115 mm
Utrecht (A.W. Bruna & Zn.)
Amsterdam, Rijksmuseum
Inv. no. RP-P-2011-125-39;
on loan from D. Bruna, Utrecht, and Mercis bv

4 Dick Bruna
cover for Georges Simenon,
Maigret aan de Rivièra
(*Maigret on the Riviera*)
1968
Relief press, 175 x 115 mm
Utrecht (A.W. Bruna & Zn.)
Amsterdam, Rijksmuseum
Inv. no. RP-D-2014-8-58;
gift of L.E. van Halem, Amsterdam, and mevrouw P.C. van Ulzen, Amsterdam

5A, B
Henri Matisse
Jazz no. 4, The Nightmare of the White Elephant, pages in the artist's book *Jazz*
1947
Letterpress, 425 x 653 mm
Lille, Palais des Beaux-Arts.
© Succession Henri Matisse, c/o Pictoright Amsterdam 2015

Henri Matisse
Jazz no. 10, The Funeral of Pierrot, pages in the artist's book *Jazz*
1947
Letterpress, 425 x 653 mm
Lille, Palais des Beaux-Arts
© Succession Henri Matisse, c/o Pictoright Amsterdam 2015

6 Dick Bruna
cover for Lizzy Sara May,
Weerzien op een plastichuid
(*Reunion on a Plasticskin*)
1957
Letterpress, 190 x 248 mm
Utrecht (A.W. Bruna & Zn.)
Amsterdam, Rijksmuseum
Inv. no. RP-P-2011-125-9;
on loan from D. Bruna, Utrecht, and Mercis bv

7 Fernand Léger
Fêtes de la faim,
in *Les Illuminations*
1949
Lithograph, 326 x 254 mm
© heirs Fernand Léger,
c/o Pictoright Amsterdam 2015

8 Dick Bruna
poster *Vakantie met een boek*
(*Holiday with a Book*)
1952
Offset, 680 x 460 mm
Utrecht (A.W. Bruna & Zn.)
Amsterdam, Stedelijk Museum
Inv. no. BT-N-154

9 Dick Bruna
cover for Shirley Jackson,
Bramen met arsenicum
(*We Have Always Lived in the Castle*)
1963
Relief press, 175 x 115 mm
Utrecht (A.W. Bruna & Zn.)

10 Willem Sandberg
cover for *Aanwinsten 1945–54. 9 jaar Stedelijk Museum*
(Acquisitions 1945–54. 9 Years Stedelijk Museum)
1945
Offset and Letterpress,
259 x 190 mm
Amsterdam, Stedelijk Museum

11 Willem Sandberg
cover for *Biblio*
1957
Lithograph and letterpress,
290 x 190 mm
Amsterdam, Stedelijk Museum
Inv. no. SA 00102(1-3)1

12A, B
Dick Bruna
cover for Bert Schierbeek,
Het boek IK (*The Book I*)
1960
Print, 175 x 115 mm
Utrecht (A.W. Bruna & Zn.)
Amsterdam, Rijksmuseum
Inv. no. RP-P-2011-125-40;
on loan from D. Bruna, Utrecht, and Mercis bv

Dick Bruna
cover for Joop van den Broek,
Steekspel in San Sebastian
(*Dual in San Sebastian*)
1961
Collage, 298 x 200 mm
Utrecht (A.W. Bruna & Zn.)
Amsterdam, Rijksmuseum
Inv. no. RP-T-2011-90-50;
on loan from D. Bruna, Utrecht, and Mercis bv

13 Dick Bruna
cover for Françoise Xenakis,
Zij zou op het eiland tegen hem zeggen (*She Would Tell Him on the Island*)
1972
Collage, 145 x 105 mm
Utrecht (A.W. Bruna & Zn.)
Amsterdam, Rijksmuseum
Inv. no. RP-T-2011-90-42;
on loan from D. Bruna, Utrecht, and Mercis bv

14 H.N. Werkman
Chassidische legenden II–10: De engel van den laatsten troost
(*Hasidic Legends II–10: The Angel of Ultimate Comfort*)
1941
Stencil print, 50.9 x 32.9 cm
Amsterdam, Stedelijk Museum
Inv. no. A 9773 [A]

15 Dick Bruna
cover for André Schwarz-Bart,
De laatste der rechtvaardigen
(*The Last of the Just*)
1961
Relief press, 210 x 320 mm
Utrecht (A.W. Bruna & Zn.)
Private collection Caro Verbeek

16 H.N. Werkman
Sabbatsgesänge
(*Sabbath Singing*)
1941
Stencil and roller on paper,
365 x 245 mm
Amsterdam, Stedelijk Museum
Inv. no. A 7821

17 Dick Bruna
cover for André Schwarz-Bart,
De laatste der rechtvaardigen
(*The Last of the Just*)
1961
Relief press, 200 x 135 mm
Utrecht (A.W. Bruna & Zn.)
Private collection Caro Verbeek

18 Dick Bruna
cover for Georges Simenon,
Maigret en het lijk zonder hoofd
(*Maigret and the Headless Corpse*)
1968
Relief press, 175 x 115 mm
Utrecht (A.W. Bruna & Zn.)
Private collection Caro Verbeek

19A, B
Dick Bruna
Twee vissen
(*Two Fish*)
1962
Monotype, 460 x 350 mm
Utrecht (A.W. Bruna & Zn.)
Amsterdam, Rijksmuseum
Inv. no. RP-P-2010-100; transfer Instituut Collectie Nederland

Georges Braque
Deux oiseaux (*Two Birds*), in the magazine *Derrière le Miroir*
1967
Offset facsimile, 383 x 560 mm
Parijs (Maeght Éditeur),
© Pictoright Amsterdam 2015

20A, B
Dick Bruna
cover design for
Sinclair Lewis, *Ann Vickers*
1950–60
Ink on paper, 90 x 125 mm
Utrecht, Centraal Museum
Inv. no. Bruna6789; Collection Centraal Museum/ illustration Dick Bruna © copyright Mercis bv, 1953–2016

Henri Matisse
La Pompadour,
from the series *Portraits*
in or after 1951–in or before 1954
Lithograph, 408 x 292 mm (sheet)
Amsterdam, Rijksmuseum
Inv. no. RP-P-2004-812; gift of E. Kotting-Menko, Amsterdam

21A, B
Dick Bruna
Still Life
1953
India ink on paper, 256 x 197 mm
Amsterdam, Rijksmuseum
Inv. no. RP-T-2011-90-23;
on loan from D. Bruna, Utrecht, and Mercis bv

Henri Matisse
Fruits, from the series
Les lithographies de l'Atelier Mourlot, Paris
1946 (design)–1964 (print)
Lithograph, 255 x 190 mm
Amsterdam, Rijksmuseum
Inv. no. RP-P-2004-654; gift of E. Kotting-Menko, Amsterdam,
© Succession H. Matisse,
c/o Pictoright Amsterdam 2015

22 Henri Matisse
Jazz no. 9, Forms, pages in the artist's book *Jazz*
1947
Silk screen in colour,
395 x 630 mm
Lille, Palais des Beaux-Arts;
© Succession H. Matisse,
c/o Pictoright Amsterdam 2015

23 Dick Bruna
designs for *de appel*
(*the apple*)
1953
Gouache, 205 x 300 mm (spread)
Amsterdam, Mercis bv

24 Dick Bruna
nijntje in het bos
(*miffy in the forest*)
2007
Silk screen in colour,
560 x 757 mm
Amsterdam, Rijksmuseum
Inv. no. RP-P-2011-125-48;
on loan from D. Bruna, Utrecht,
and Mercis bv

25A, B
Dick Bruna
cover of *de appel*
(*the apple*)
1953 (first edition)
Relief press, 205 x 150 mm
Amsterdam, Mercis bv

Dick Bruna
cover of *de appel*
(*the apple*)
1959
Relief press, 160 x 160 mm
Amsterdam, Mercis bv

26 Henri Matisse
design for stained-glass
window for the Chapelle
du Rosaire in Vence
1951
© Succession H. Matisse,
c/o Pictoright Amsterdam 2015

27 Henri Matisse
detail of second design for
stained-glass window for the
Chapelle du Rosaire in Vence
1951
© Succession H. Matisse,
c/o Pictoright Amsterdam 2015

28 Henri Matisse
The Sheaf
1953
Cut-out, 294 x 350 cm
Los Angeles, Collection
University of California,
Hammer Museum; gift of
Mr. and Mrs. Sidney F. Brody,
© Succession H. Matisse,
c/o Pictoright Amsterdam 2015

29 Dick Bruna
Miffy and Matisse,
in *nijntje in het museum*
(*miffy at the gallery*)
1997
Letterpress, 160 x 160 mm
Amsterdam, Mercis bv

30 Dick Bruna
cover for Leslie Charteris,
De Saint wordt piraat
(*The Pirate Saint*)
1961
Print on cardboard, 175 x 115 mm
Utrecht (A.W. Bruna & Zn.)
Private collection Caro Verbeek

31 Dick Bruna
cover design for *de brief*
van nijntje (*miffy's letter*)
2003
Collage with film removed,
160 x 160 mm
Amsterdam, Rijksmuseum
Inv. no. RP-P-2011-125-18;
on loan from D. Bruna, Utrecht,
and Mercis bv

32 Bart van der Leck
Composition
(Milkmaid with a Cow)
c. 1921
Lithograph, 355 x 458 mm
Amsterdam, Rijksmuseum
Inv. no. RP-P-1936-447;
F.G. Waller Bequest, Amsterdam,
© Pictoright Amsterdam 2015

33A, B
Gerrit Rietveld
Armchair for Til Brugman
c. 1919 (design)–1923 (execution)
Painted wood, 87 x 65.5 x 84 cm
Amsterdam, Rijksmuseum
Inv. no. BK-2010-1; purchased
with the support of the
BankGiro Loterij, © heirs of
Gerrit Rietveld, c/o Pictoright
Amsterdam 2015

Gerrit Rietveld
Side Table for Til Brugman
1923
Multiplex, 61.5 x 49 x 49 cm
Amsterdam, Rijksmuseum
Inv. no. BK-C-2013-4; on loan
from C. Oetker, Frankfurt am
Main, © heirs of Gerrit Rietveld,
c/o Pictoright Amsterdam 2015

34 Willem Sandberg
Kwadraat-blad (*Square Page*)
1966
Offset, 249 x 249 mm
Amsterdam (De Jong & Co.)
Amsterdam, Stedelijk Museum
Inv. no. 2004.1.0474

35 Dick Bruna
cover of *nijntje aan zee*
(*miffy at the seaside*)
1996
Letterpress, 160 x 160 mm
Amsterdam, Mercis bv

36A, B
Dick Bruna
detail of Miffy and De Stijl,
in *nijntje in het museum*
(*miffy at the gallery*)
1997
Letterpress, 160 x 160 mm
Amsterdam, Mercis bv

Dick Bruna
Miffy and De Stijl,
in *nijntje in het museum*
(*miffy at the gallery*)
1997
Letterpress, 160 x 160 mm
Amsterdam, Mercis bv

37 Piet Mondrian
Picture No. III; Lozenge
Composition with Eight Lines
and Red
1938
Oil on canvas, 100.5 x 100.5 cm
Riehen/Basel, Fondation
Beyeler, Beyeler Collection
Inv. no. Welsh/Joosten B 282

38 Theo van Doesburg
Contra-Composition V
1924
Oil on canvas, 100 x 100 cm
Amsterdam, Stedelijk Museum
Inv. no. A 567

39 Dick Bruna
Miffy writing, sketch for
de brief van nijntje
(*miffy's letter*)
2003
Pencil on transparent paper,
296 x 177 mm
Amsterdam, Rijksmuseum
Inv. no. RP-T-2011-90-90;
on loan from D. Bruna, Utrecht,
and Mercis bv

40 Dick Bruna
Miffy writing, study for
de brief van nijntje
(*miffy's letter*)
2003
Collage and film, 160 x 160 mm
Amsterdam, Rijksmuseum
Inv. no. RP-P-2011-125-18;
on loan from D. Bruna, Utrecht,
and Mercis bv

41 Dick Bruna
Miffy writing, cover design for
de brief van nijntje
(*miffy's letter*)
2003
Gouache, 160 x 160 mm
Amsterdam, Rijksmuseum
Inv. no. RP-T-2011-90-52;
on loan from D. Bruna, Utrecht,
and Mercis bv

42 Dick Bruna
Miffy and friend in the water,
design for *de brief van nijntje*
(*miffy's letter*)
2003
160 x 160 mm
Amsterdam, Rijksmuseum
Inv. no. RP-P-2011-125-24

43 Dick Bruna
dinner plate, design for
de brief van nijntje
(*miffy's letter*)
2003
160 x 160 mm
Amsterdam Rijksmuseum
Inv. no. RP-P-2011-125-27

44 Dick Bruna
Miffy and friends dancing,
design for *de brief van nijntje*
(*miffy's letter*)
2003
160 x 160 mm
Amsterdam, Rijksmuseum
Inv. no. RP-P-2011-125-19

45 Dick Bruna
cover of *nijntje* (*miffy*)
book 16
1963
Letterpress, 160 x 160 mm
Amsterdam, Mercis bv

46 Dick Bruna
pages from the first
Miffy publication
book 1
1955
Letterpress, 120 x 220 mm
Amsterdam, Mercis bv

47 Dick Bruna
Miffy and Calder,
in *nijntje in het museum*
(*miffy at the gallery*):
1997
Letterpress, 160 x 160 mm
Amsterdam, Mercis bv

48 Rijksmuseum curators drew
the eyes and cross in the
outline of Miffy's face

49 Dick Bruna
Miffy and her mother,
in *nijntje in het museum*
(*miffy at the gallery*)
1997
Letterpress, 160 x 160 mm
Amsterdam, Mercis bv

50A, B
Dick Bruna
off to the museum and
walking back home,
in *nijntje in het museum*
(*miffy at the gallery*)
1997
Letterpress, 160 x 160 mm
Amsterdam, Mercis bv

51A, B
Dick Bruna
Miffy on the look-out and
Miffy stealing, in *nijntje is stout*
(*miffy is naughty*)
2007
Letterpress, 160 x 160 mm
Amsterdam, Mercis bv

52 Dick Bruna
Miffy in bed, in *nijntje is stout*
(*miffy is naughty*)
2007
Letterpress, 160 x 160 mm
Amsterdam, Mercis bv

53 Dick Bruna
Miffy crying over the loss of
her teddybear, in *nijntje huilt*
(*miffy is crying*)
1991
Letterpress, 160 x 160 mm
Amsterdam, Mercis bv

54 Dick Bruna
Miffy crying over her
grandmother's death,
in *lieve oma pluis*
(*dear grandma bunny*)
1996
Letterpress, 160 x 160 mm
Amsterdam, Mercis bv

55 Dick Bruna
Miffy and apple,
in *nijntje in het museum*
(*miffy at the gallery*)
1997
Letterpress, 160 x 160 mm
Amsterdam, Mercis bv

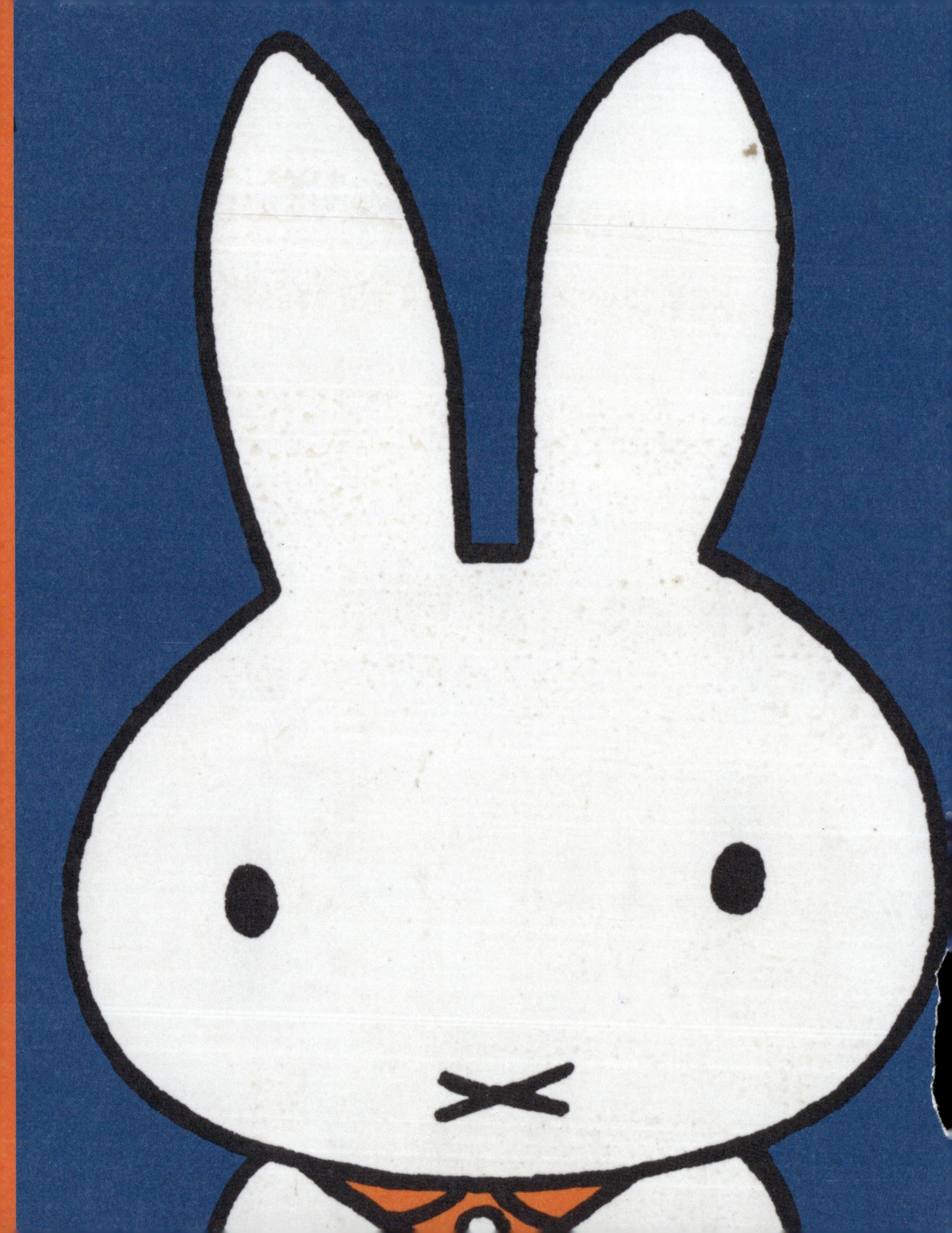